Re-scheduling Televi
in the Digital Era

This book explores how the television industry is adapting its production culture and professional practices of scheduling to an increasingly non-linear television paradigm. Centered around four case studies, the book argues that a new television paradigm is being produced from within the multiplatform television organizations themselves in order to adapt to changing viewer habits and to the tensions between digital and broadcast television.

Drawing on a unique genre and production studies approach, the analysis includes in-depth studies of:

- The communicative changes to the on-air schedule as a televisual text phenomenon in the digital era, and how the conceptualizations of the audience are changing in scheduling and curation for multiplatform portfolios;
- The changing production culture of scheduling in companies for their multiplatform portfolios;
- The dilemmas of curation in multiplatform portfolios.

Situated at the intersection of the humanities and sociology in media production studies, this book will be of key interest to scholars and students of television studies, media production studies and cultural studies and to researchers and media professionals and management in the television industry.

Hanne Bruun is Professor of Media Studies at Aarhus University, Denmark. She is the founder and head of the Centre for Media Industries and Production Studies; the author of four books, including *Dansk tv-satire. Underholdning med kant*; and the co-editor of four books. She has contributed to several books, e.g. *Advancing Media Production Studies* eds. Paterson, C. et al., and journals, e.g. *Nordic Journal of Media Studies*, *Critical Studies in Television*, *Nordicom Review*, the *European Journal of Communication* and *Media, Culture & Society*.

Routledge Focus on Television Studies

The Evolution of Black Women in Television
Mammies, Matriarchs and Mistresses
Imani M. Cheers

Heroism, Celebrity and Therapy in Nurse Jackie
Christopher Pullen

Re-scheduling Television in the Digital Era
Hanne Bruun

Re-scheduling Television in the Digital Era

Hanne Bruun

Routledge
Taylor & Francis Group

LONDON AND NEW YORK

First published 2020
by Routledge
2 Park Square, Milton Park, Abingdon, Oxon OX14 4RN

and by Routledge
605 Third Avenue, New York, NY 10017

First issued in paperback 2022

Routledge is an imprint of the Taylor & Francis Group, an informa business

Library of Congress Cataloging-in-Publication Data
A catalog record has been requested for this book

ISBN: 978-1-03-240089-1 (pbk)
ISBN: 978-0-367-22675-6 (hbk)
ISBN: 978-0-429-27630-9 (ebk)

DOI: 10.4324/9780429276309

Typeset in Times New Roman
by codeMantra

For Bille Bruun Helles

Contents

Illustrations

Figures

Tables

Acknowledgements

This book is about the television schedule and its production, and it is about the present changes to this TV genre, which features characteristics fundamental to what is understood as 'television' among researchers, even if the academic interest has been very spare. The book goes back to 2014 and highlights the developments in Danish television between 2014 and 2019. It tries to keep a balance between change and continuity in an apparently volatile industry, and my hope is that the findings will contribute to at least a heuristic conceptualisation of the schedule and scheduling in the digital era. The idea for this book came out of a long 'love affair' with television as a medium and many years of research on its different genres and audiences, as well as the industrial and cultural-political contexts that shape the ways in which the medium works and develops. For the last 15 years my research interests have made me focus on an approach in the broader field of media studies, termed media industry and media production studies. Within this approach I have been especially interested in the way in which the genres of television structure and frame the way in which television content is produced and how the professional work of television production changes over time. While working on this book between 2013 and 2019, I have been teaching a master course: *Television and Television Theory in the Digital Era* at the MA programme in Media Studies at Aarhus University. The students have been part of helping this book along, and I would like to thank all of them, especially the class of 2019, who acted as guinea pigs reading and commenting on the different chapters of the book.

I find myself very fortunate that several of my clever and supportive colleagues at the Centre for Media Industries and Production as well as members of the research programme *Media, Communication and Society* at Aarhus University share interests similar to mine

(Anne Marit Waade, Pia Majbritt Jensen, Eva Novrup Redvall, Henrik Bødker, Per Jauert, Jakob Isak Nielsen, Susanne Eichner, and Niels Brügger). We have had some very important research seminars and informal discussions over the last five years, during which I have been researching, presenting drafts and writing this book. Particular thanks must be given for the academic and moral support as well as the invaluable critical feedback I received from my colleague Professor Kirsten Frandsen, with whom I have written many papers and articles, and edited four books over the years. The value of collaborative work is also underpinned by the academic network I have been part of in the *European Communication Research and Education Association* (ECREA) section *Media Industries and Cultural Production* and in the *Television* section at the *NordMedia* conferences during recent years. Special thanks go to Professor David Hesmondhalgh and Professor Catherine Johnson for their interest in my work and helpful support.

I would not have been able to write this book without the help of the many media professionals in the Danish Television industry who were kind enough to participate in interviews about how the production of a schedule is done and what the work of a scheduler, a continuity producer or a promotion producer is. Without academic access to the industry and its professional practices, media studies would not be able to remain in proper touch with its objects of study, and I am extremely grateful to the 20 individuals that participated in formal interviews and for their informal talks and correspondence with me, and their giving me the opportunity to observe the kind of work they do. I am particularly grateful to the Head of Scheduling at TV 2 Mette, Rysø Johansen, and Head of TV 2 Play, Kurt Holm Jensen, for their interest in helping me many times and commenting on my work; I hope to continue our knowledge exchange and discussions in the future. Writing a book takes up a lot of one's time and energy, and I am very grateful to friends and family, who patiently listened to my endless chatter about the schedule and television. Special thanks must go to my husband Allan for putting up with me for the last several months, a period during which we also became grandparents to the most wonderful baby boy, to whom I dedicated this book. As I put on the finishing touches, the birth and first few months of Bille Bruun Helles's life has made me begin to comprehend one of life's true miracles.

Finally, I would like to thank the editors at Routledge for their editorial help and for fast tracking this book. Three of its seven chapters are building on previously published works: Chapter 3 is building on empirical results previously published in *Nordicom Review* 37(2) 2016.

Chapter 4 is an updated and edited version of 'The Delay Economy of "Continuity"' published in *Nordic Journal of Media Studies* 2019, 1(1). Chapter 5 is building on empirical results previously published in *Critical Studies in Television* 13(2) 2018. I would like to thank the publishers, Nordicom and Sage, for allowing this and for acknowledging that the production of knowledge in academia in the digital era needs to be free of restrictive copyright regulations.

1 What is the schedule, and why study it?

Introduction

I am sitting in my living room on a Saturday at 7.53 pm 29th of September 2018. Together with my husband, and a lot of other Danes we are watching television and waiting for the Danish version of the British reality game show *The Big Bake Off* to start. The show has been a big hit for DR1, the main channel of the Danish public service radio and television company DR, and DR is about to air its 7th season of the show and has moved the show from Monday at 8 pm to Saturday. The few minutes of television that we are watching before the show starts is not scheduled in the online TV guide we use, but it is a very familiar and common part of the daily experience of being a television viewer. What we witness is a channel voice greeting us and building expectations towards the show that is about to start "in a moment" while showing a trailer from the upcoming episode. The channel voice goes on to tell us what DR has to offer on 3 of its other 5 channels "right now" showing trailers for these programmes. This is followed by the promotion and a trailer for the upcoming Danish drama series on DR1 later this Fall. The speak and trailers that offers us to see something else now or later on another channel is topped by the information that DR's streaming service DRTV offers us a preview of the next episode of a documentary on DR3, DR's youth channel. The DR1 channel voice then finally announces that *The Big Bake Off* is starting, and the show begins. If we had turned on one of the commercially funded channels instead of DR that is financed by a media tax, we would have been asked to wait while the commercials were shown as well as all the announcements of the different sponsors involved in financing the programme we were about to watch.

The situation described above is probably very familiar to everyone watching traditional linear television now-a-days, and the piece of television content experienced is a bit of the so-called on-air schedule and 'continuity,' which is the industry term for the bits in between the programmes. In television studies, the schedule, including the on-air schedule and 'continuity,' is fundamental to what is understood as a key characteristic of television as a time structured medium and to how the everyday life of the audience and the medium is intertwined. The schedule is perhaps even one of the most distinctive features of television as a medium. It not only creates a setting for the individual programmes but is also a communicative interface between the television channel, the company and the viewers. The schedule is a prism of current changes to television and a playground for navigating these changes within the industry. In this book I argue that research on the on-air schedule and on scheduling is more important than ever because it is much more than the distribution of content. It is communication and relationship building with an audience. The book joins forces with a new wave of scholarly interest emerging especially in Europe because of the tradition for public service television, and it is connected to a broader set of changes to television in the digital era. Since the arrival of broadband internet, the access to high-speed web connections in households and on mobile devices, and the possibility to distribute audio-visual content over the public internet the incumbent television industry is moving into a transitional period that is changing the schedule as a genre and how it is produced. Interactive social media like YouTube and on demand services like Netflix, Amazon Prime and HBO have enhanced the viewers' control of what to watch, and of, when and where they watch television. Watching television does not have to take place on a television set and has become much more independent of the time structures of the schedule compared to what was possible using the Digital Video Recorders (DVR) and previously remote controls. The content is mobile in terms of devices and location, and the programmes do not need to be embedded in the timeliness of a schedule in order to reach an audience. The content is accessible as files in databases that are interactively connected to the users and respond to this specific use in different ways using algorithms. The content does not need to fit the slot structures of a schedule that is mirroring and shaping the temporal structures of everyday life but is shaped by what Johnson (2019) terms 'frames that organise content within services and devices and shape how it is experienced' (p. 9). To sum up, scheduling is currently marked by the tensions between a familiar linear television paradigm and an emerging non-linear television paradigm, and at least these five key characteristics of the two paradigms collide (Table 1.1):

Table 1.1 Two television paradigms

Television paradigm	Linear	Non-linear
1: Consumption	Central locality and the TV-set	Multiple localities and digital devices
2: Viewer access	Time structured access to content	On-demand access to content
3: Communication	One-way and mass communication	Interactivity
4: Textual characteristics: distribution	Schedules and content mirroring and structuring the temporal structures of everyday life of an audience	Spatial structures and files in databases
5: Textual characteristics: content	Temporal standardisation of content to fit distribution structures	No fixed temporal logics

The schedule, including the on-air schedule and 'continuity,' can be regarded as a 'child' of these key characteristics of the linear television paradigm outlined above and its industrial logics. An important part of these industrial logics is the dominating business model in the television industry: the commercial break. As an integrated part of the on-air schedule and 'continuity' this business model is presently challenged as part of the tensions between a linear and a non-linear television paradigm. This means that the non-linear paradigm potentially upsets the schedule as a point of connection between the communicative, industrial and cultural-political dimensions of television's role in a society. These dimensions are potentially at stake, and this book is an investigation of how the television companies navigate in the tensions between the two paradigms, and its focus is on how the work influences the role of the schedule and of scheduling as a professional craft.

The television industry in many countries all over the world is marked by this technological disruption and it is safe to say that understanding television and the television industry in the digital era is a work still in progress in television studies. Among others, Amanda Lotz's work based on the development of the television industry in the United States has been very important and influential. Lotz argues that the television industry in the United States is currently in a historic phase of transition on the route towards a so-called post-network era (Lotz 2014: 21–32). Furthermore, drawing on Bernard Miege's three models of media production logics, Lotz argues that the flow model typical for radio and television industries is giving way to a publishing model best known from the film, music and book publishing industries (Lotz 2017: 7–10). Even if there certainly is very hard evidence of fundamental changes taking place in the television industry in Lotz's work, these assumptions are based on a rather linear and simplistic notion of how media development works, and second they are reflecting the commercial context of the North American media system. As suggested by Grainge and Johnson (2018) based on their analysis of the managerial discourse on the BBC iPlayer understanding the development of the television industry in the digital era needs some further discussions based on findings from research on how the television industry develops in media systems *outside* of the United States. Enli and Syvertsen argue that it is generally needed to include political and cultural factors in the analysis of how television is developing (Enli and Syvertsen 2016). Especially the political tradition of elaborated cultural-political regulation and subsidies on a national and international level must be considered, as well as the priority given to well-funded public service obligated television broadcasters in the North-Western European and Nordic countries. Furthermore, the 'media ecosystem' (ibid.: 147) in different markets is important and especially the balance between private and public media.

The television industry in the Nordic countries is first of all defined by a very strong public media sector, and even within this context the television industry in Denmark stands out. The two television companies, TV 2 and the Danish Radio and Television Company (DR), both with public service obligations, dominate the television market with a combined share of viewing of 76 per cent in 2018 compared to a combined share of viewing of 65 per cent between BBC, ITV and Channel4 in the United Kingdom (BARB 2019: 28). This strong market position frames how commercial television companies try to navigate in order to get a piece of the pie on a market with a decline in traditional television viewing. Both companies have a platform neutral obligation to inform, enlighten and entertain. Especially it is a paramount obligation to offer a population of 5.6 million people a substantial production of Danish-language content across genres and subject areas in order to join the citizens in small and large communities (*DR's Public Service Kontrakt 2019–2023; Tilladelse til TV 2 Danmark 2019-2013*). Currently around 70 per cent of the content is in Danish (2018). DR's streaming service DRTV is included in the licence fee that will gradually be turned into a media tax by 2022. TV 2 is funded by subscription and commercials, and the basic version including commercials of the subscription-based streaming service TV 2 Play is included, if TV 2 is part of a bundled cable television subscription provided by the telecom companies. If not, TV 2 Play is as a stand-alone service in different versions on the internet. A more elaborated account of the Danish television market, the major companies and regulatory regime will follow in Chapter 3, but for now and to sum up, the industrial and cultural-political dimensions of the schedule and of scheduling are very visible given the public service obligations and the popularity of public service television. For public service television the challenge facing scheduling is to maintain this market position and to meet the obligations in the tensions between the two paradigms.

The second reason for looking into how scheduling develops using the Danish television market as a case has to do with the fact that Denmark is part of the 'avant-garde' in terms of being an actual digital society (*DESI/Digital Economy and Society Index 2019*, European Commission, 2019). Google and Apple are using Denmark as a datacentre hub because of its digital infrastructures, low energy prices, green energy supply and stable political environment (Oxvig 2018). The changes to the television industry by the emerging non-linear paradigm are supported by the fact that 99 per cent of households have internet access and 93 per cent have high-speed broadband access (2019). Furthermore, the use of mobile broadband is on the increase and in 2018 Denmark had the highest 4G coverage in Europe, and in 2019 the 5G started to be rolled out. In terms of digital devices 61 per cent of the households have a smart TV, and 88 per cent have a smart phone (Agency of Culture and Palaces *Mediernes udvikling i Danmark – Internetbrug og enheder* 2019: 22). Based on these conditions, the viewing habits in the population are changing fast and 53 per cent of the Danes (12+) stream from the broadcaster's services every week and 40 per cent use Netflix every week (2018). Young segments of the population are spearheading this development, and the changing viewer habits will be elaborated in Chapter 4. However, the older segments of the population are following in their footsteps at a high rate which will gradually close the alleged generational gab. 98 per cent of the 12–34-year-old and 88 per cent of the 35–54-year-old stream every month. A rising number of the 55–70-year-old are doing the same, from 55 per cent in 2017 to 62 per cent in 2018, and the use among the +71-year-old rose from 31 to 34 per cent. (Agency of Culture and Palaces *Mediernes udvikling i Danmark: Streaming - Audiovisual Services* 2018: 10).

Based on these two characteristics the question is what happens to television scheduling in a television market where the non-linear use of television is increasing, which is strongly supported by the mature digital infrastructure and the cultural policies regulating a dominating public service sector? And furthermore, what happens to scheduling in a market where the use of international streaming services like Netflix is rapidly becoming a mainstream activity among the viewers but where public service television is still very popular compared to commercial television, and where fairly traditional public service obligations and business models are still in place? The book uses the, in many ways, *extreme case* of the television industry in Denmark to illuminate and discuss how the television schedule and scheduling as well as television in general are developing in the tensions between two television paradigms that in many ways collide. The idea is that the combination of a very small, public service television dominated and digitally advance market makes the study able to unlock empirical perspective and a broader set of issues around scheduling, the future of the television industry and especially public service television's ability to attract an audience. This book will add to the confusion and insecurities about the future of television within the industry and in television studies by suggesting that a *third television paradigm* is presently being produced by television companies. The companies are faced with the new competitors like YouTube and Netflix, and they are changing from within by including streaming services in their portfolios in different ways. The companies are in that sense not just to be regarded as objects of change in the industry but are powerful agents of change themselves trying to ensure their own individual survival as a company and in some cases to meet cultural-political obligations too. The book traces how these changes and adaption played out based on findings from 2014 to 2019, a period when Netflix became a serious competitor and the focus of the television companies shifted from cross-media production towards non-linear production and distribution.

The functions and tiers of the schedule

In this book the schedule is regarded as the point of connection between industrial and cultural-political dimensions, and the historical development of the schedule as a competitive tool is where changes in the television industry become very visible. This role as a prism of change has to do with the fact that in traditional linear television the schedule performs five communicative functions on-air between the programmes that create the interface between the company and the viewers:

1   The on-air schedule has to inform the viewers of upcoming content, retain the viewers' attention during these intermissions and

even attract new users. The text produced must tackle the tension between, on the one hand, the schedule and the programmes, and, on the other hand, the time viewers spend waiting for the next programme to begin. In short, it needs to *inform* and to *entertain* in order to control and secure an audience flow. In public service television the schedule additionally has to meet cultural-political demands to make television a significant source of information, enlightenment and entertainment, and to support a cultural and political democracy. As a consequence, the public service companies aim to construct channel schedules that will make the viewers watch specific and/or a variety of genres, e.g. by placing the news before or after popular entertainment shows, or by offering niche channels for special target groups, e.g. young people. Internal diversity and a mixed menu are part of the normative ideal guiding the production of the schedule and implicitly the conceptualisation of the audience.

2   The on-air schedule is where the provider explicitly tries to *brand itself* and its products (Stigel 2004, 2006). It is where the quintessence of the specific 'house style' (Ellis 1982) of the provider's portfolio of channels, platforms and content is presented in the interstitials of 'continuity.'

3   The on-air schedule is where the dominant *business model* of commercially financed, linear television (with or without public service obligations) unfolds, in the guise of advertisements and sponsorship announcements, as breaks either within or between the programmes. The audience is the commodity sold to advertisers on the basis of audience measurement data for the channel(s) and its programmes, and the television schedule must provide a suitable environment for these commercial messages. In this way scheduling needs to optimise the company's programming resources for individual channels and overall portfolios. Only the very few 100 per cent non-commercially funded television companies in the world, like the BBC, SVT, NRK and DR, do not rely on this business model to some degree.

4   In the kind of communicative interface constructed by the interstitials of 'continuity,' we also find the quintessence of the *immediacy and 'live-ness' of the television experience* as a time-structured mass medium (Williams 1974; Ellis 1982). A perpetual 'here and now' is presented, first, in which the different parts of the day (daytime, prime time, late fringe) and the week are mirrored, and, second, to which the different temporal and spatial settings of the individual programmes (e.g. the here-and-now of the talk show;

the there-and-now of the television transmission of an event; the there-and-then of the television drama) return (Stigel 2001).

5   It is in the communicative interface built by 'continuity' that the *acknowledgement of the viewers' presence* is persistently recognised. 'Continuity' is probably an important component of the 'anyone as someone' structure of the television experience that Scannell defines, interlinking the private sphere of the viewer(s) and the public sphere of television in everyday life (Scannell 1996: 14). In this way, 'continuity' is probably a fundamental component of the 'taken-for-granted-ness' and 'dailiness' of television, as Scannell argues (1996: 9, 144). Furthermore, the schedule and 'continuity' bear witness to a conceptualisation of the audience and the everyday life and possible tastes, interests and needs of this implied audience. The schedule has to address this context build and sustain viewing habits.

To sum up, the schedule merges communication, commercial needs and cultural-political obligations, and of course distribution of the programmes. In this book I argue theoretically and empirically that it is fruitful to regard the schedule as a *specific televisual genre*. At first, this approach might seem a bit controversial to a phenomenon that is often regarded as 'just' distribution or 'frames' organising the real content of television: the programmes. However, in Chapter 2 I argue that the schedule is a genre in its own right. First, it is a televisual *text* produced by professionals just like the news, the quiz shows, the television fiction series and all the other genres of television. This text has a long history in television and is influenced by the different political and cultural contexts surrounding television. Second, it is recognised as a specific kind of text by the producers and the audience alike, and from their different perspective the two parties expect the text to perform the communicative functions described above.

Regarded as a televisual text the schedule is made up of three tiers. First, it is constructed by the different kinds of programmes and films that each of the television companies offer their intended audiences on the different channels and platforms in their portfolios. This can be equated with the kind of products that a supermarket has decided to have on its shelves for its customers. The second tier of what constitutes the schedule is the vertical and horizontal time structures that place the programmes in a strategic order of succession. This means, for example, organising what will be on the main channel on Monday nights at 7 pm after the news cast and before the current affairs series at 8:30 pm during the winter season. Here the different time zones of the schedule are planned to communicate with the everyday life of the audience and the competition in the market. These time zones are called 'slots,' and in the struggle to retain the audience for a longer period of time and attract specific target groups, the location of a programme in the schedule can be important to its success as well as its failure. The third tier of what constitutes the schedule is the final broadcast of the schedule: the on-air schedule described above. It includes not only the programmes in their particular order but also the interstitials called 'continuity' as well as commercials and sponsorship announcements that are placed between the programmes or parts of the programmes. The interstitials are a mixture of para-texts like trailers, banners, channel logos and schedule outlines, as well as channel voice address and different kinds of audio-visual separators. The on-air schedule is also the top level of television's discursive hierarchy where the television company explicitly addresses its audiences in the guise of the channel voice. The on-air schedule is the 'supertext' of the television medium as Nick Browne has termed it (Browne 1984: 176), and the kind of organisational or corporate identity that the viewers meet when they watch several programmes across linear television. The on-air schedule is also described as 'the architecture that combines them [the programme genres of television]' (Ellis 2000a: 131), as a junction using a montage of 'interstitials' (Ellis 2011; Johnson 2013) and as a montage of 'paratexts' (Gray 2010). Ellis describes the work of the producers of this text as 'editing on an Olympian scale' (2000b: 25), defining a specific broadcast television service and making it distinguishable from other services. In this sense, the on-air schedule is important as a branding tool in a competitive television market (Johnson 2012).

The production process behind the schedule that finally goes on-air and hits the screen can be broken down into the same stages that structure a live television production genre like the news cast, but with a *very* different time frame. The daily broadcast of the on-air schedule is the result of a preproduction process extending up to three years into the future. This preproduction process involves constant adjustments and re-editing of the planned schedule, which is optimised until it is broadcast. Today this process typically involves a number of computer systems in which adjustments are implemented, and the final product constitutes a so-called 'playlist' for the daily broadcast. The playlist contains all the programmes and interstitials produced in a time schedule and must be followed by the live broadcast producer during transmission of the content. This phase of the preproduction process involves monitoring audience ratings and competitors closely as well as events in the outside world. An unexpected event in the outside world can be a total game changer, which means that the playlist has to be profoundly re-edited, with all the promotional work already done being, at worst, wasted. An example of this profound influence on the playlist happened during my stay at the television company TV 2 in Denmark in the early spring of 2016, when a political crisis almost caused a call for a general election. This was going on during the broadcasting of a high-priority promotional campaign in the on-air schedule, and on other platforms, for a broadcast of a prime-time documentary serial for the main channel. The serial was highly controversial in its methods and aimed to expose the influence the imams allegedly have in the Muslim community in Denmark. If the crisis had resulted in a call for a general election, the promotional campaign would have been wasted, because TV 2 would have had to reschedule the serial for political reasons. TV 2's main channel has public service obligations connected to its broadcasting licence and broadcasting the serial would have been considered biased during a general election where issues on integration and migration would have been high on the agenda for all political parties in Denmark.

Even if the schedule, the on-air-schedule as an interface and the many communicative functions performed by 'continuity,' television studies have been strangely indifferent to this specific televisual genre as well as to scheduling as a craft performed by professional continuity producers and schedulers. The scholarly interest is dwarfed by the overwhelming interest among the researchers, myself included, in doing programme and genres analysis, audience studies and more general television industry studies. These approaches have dominated television studies in the past and continue to do so. The importance of the schedule and of scheduling is, however, acknowledged in television studies, and the interest in the schedule as a text and in doing scheduling studies has surfaced twice since the early 1970s. The first ripple of academic interest is visible in connections with the basic reflections on what characterises television as a medium compared to other cultural forms or media. In his seminal work Raymond Williams's (1974) conceptualisation of television as a 'flow' was argued using the results from a comparative analysis of the schedules from British public service television and commercial television in the United States. Williams argued that broadcasting as the new communication technology introduced a fundamentally different temporality in consuming cultural goods, and as a consequence a new cultural experience was made possible. The discrete forms of e.g. the lecture, the concert, the theatrical play or the cinema would all be connected in the linear organisation of the on-air schedule that aimed to dissolve the differences between them into *one* seamless experience of watching television. In 1978 Fiske and Hartley's definition of the television medium briefly used the on-air schedule as part of their argument for television's semiotic, ritualistic and bardic functions in society (1978/2004: 134). In line with this theoretical framing, the function of 'continuity' was likened to a boundary ritual that separates the programmes and the editorial material from the commercial breaks. Compared to this approach to the schedule Nick Brown's work from 1984 is based on a political economy approach and is taking on a more focussed and systematic analysis. The argument is that an analysis of the schedule will contribute to understand the medium in general and its role in society:

> An analysis of the schedule would allow us to identify the main lines of television programming – the rise and fall of genre, format, personalities, and the migration and iterations of form – and to begin the process of charting the terms and contours of an institutional, as well as social, history of television. I mean then to put the analysis of the history, logic, and form of the schedule on the new agenda of contemporary television theory.
>
> (Brown 1984: 177)

However, television studies did not take the bait until the profound changes in the television industry during the late 1980s and 1990s in Europe became important to investigate. Satellite technology supported distribution of transnational television and a wave of deregulation of television in Europe followed resulting in the growing competition between private and public service television companies and growing portfolios. This development made scheduling a more complex task and a small wavelet of interest in studying scheduling and 'continuity' emerged in the light of these fundamental changes. The focus was on how European public service television tried to adapt to this new television market. The contributions by Ellis (2000a, 2000b) and Paterson (1990) on British television, and by Søndergaard (1994, 2003) and Ytreberg (2002) on Danish and Norwegian public service television show how the communicative characteristics of the schedule and scheduling became increasingly important. These contributions drew on results from a business, marketing and media management studies approach to the American television industry since the 1970s. This small contingent of research was and still is typically measuring and testing the viability and commercial efficiency of different tactics, e.g. counter-programming, lead-in tactics (Tiedge and Ksobiech 1986, 1987; Reddy et al. 1998). It addresses scheduling as a craft and with a professional set of terms attached to this craft, e.g. 'tentpoling,' 'hammocking,' and 'stripping' (Howard et al. 1994; Eastman and Ferguson 2009, 2013). As pointed out by Søndergaard (2003) the communicative strategies of public service broadcasters became very similar to those of commercial channels during the 1990s. Furthermore, the increasing focus on the schedule as a competitive tool changed the organisational structures and production modes in the public service companies, and this, in turn, changed their conceptualisation of the audience. A far more systematic use of ratings and socio-demographic segmentation tools were implemented in the work of the schedulers pointing towards viewers as lifestyle segments and consumers with different needs and tastes that had to be met. During the 1990s the schedulers became part of the top management of the television companies. The importance of the schedule and the editorial power of scheduling were acknowledged and this only increased during the late 1990s and the first ten years of the new millennium when the channel portfolios of the television companies proliferated. The current development in the television industry is accelerating the complexity of scheduling, and this book will contribute to the investigation of how important aspects of the schedule and the production culture of scheduling develop based on empirical material from 2014 to 2019. However, the speed of change in the industry is a problem for doing research and writing a book like this. First, the empirical facts and concrete situations change rapidly which the temporalities of research and academic publishing are not able to match. Second, the volatility in the industry means that the focus of the book is on how disruption and sustainability play out, and it applies a relatively heuristic perspective to this ongoing process of transformation.

The outline of the book

Apart from this introductory chapter the book is divided into six chapters. Chapter 2 starts off by presenting the emerging wave of scholarly interest in the schedule and in scheduling because of the growth of non-linear television and the many questions this development poses to what television is and its role in society. I argue an approach to both the schedule as a text and scheduling as a professional skill in the industry based on a pragmatic and socio-cognitive understanding of genre. According to this approach there is a reciprocal relationship between the genre produced and the developments in specific professional media production cultures. The theoretical approach has the ability to highlight the interplay between human agency and different kinds of structural and technological forces. Second, the approach has the potential to integrate media texts and especially the micro- and meso-levels of production, which is fruitful in order to understand the way the television industry navigates in the tensions between the two television paradigms. The second part of Chapter 2 reviews the different kinds of knowledge of the audience (quantitative, qualitative and cultural knowledge) implemented in television scheduling. These sources of knowledge are, however, rooted in the linear television paradigm, and this 'exposure model' (Johnson 2019: 137) is challenged by the promise of personalisation based on algorithms.

Chapter 3 starts with a brief introduction to the Danish television industry, and to the regulatory framework. This is needed in order to contextualise the analysis of the changing communicative behaviour in 'continuity' produced by public service companies. Based on a case study of the main channels of DR and TV 2 in Denmark, the chapter suggests that an increasing *divergence* marks the development in the digital era between the two providers. Three major differences are found in the efforts to, first, retain and to 'herd' the viewers within the scope of products; second, to strengthen the provider-viewer relationship; and, third, to stand out with a distinct set of institutional values. The chapter concludes that the findings can be regarded as a consequence of the challenges and opportunities facing these institutions in terms of funding and in terms of meeting public service obligations that navigate the tension between a linear and a non-linear television paradigm. This is elaborated further in Chapter 4 that questions, compares and discusses the survivability of the kind of 'continuity' produced by private and public service television companies in the digital era from the perspective of the audience and the changing viewer habits. The focus is on the four major companies on the Danish market: Nordic Entertainment Group (NENT), Discovery, DR and TV 2. The chapter shows that a very traditional *delay economy* is still governing the temporal structures and constructions of 'continuity' that draws heavily on the patience of its implied viewer. Especially the private television companies display a very conservative strategy, and divergence between public service and private television is blatant. Subsequently, the chapter argues that the present media environment in which the companies are embedded is marked by an emerging impatience culture. A new viewer mentality might be evolving based on instant access to personalised audio-visual content and experiences with digital games on different devices. The chapter concludes that this viewer mentality presently evolving is a challenge to the survivability of 'continuity' and its delay economy. However, the scheduling strategies also bear witness to the resilience of the linear television paradigm in an industry producing its own future in which the linear and the non-linear are intertwined.

In the following two chapters the book investigates the *production* of the schedule. Chapter 5 presents results from a production study on how on-air scheduling as a craft is changing in the digital era. The company in focus of the case study is the Danish commercially funded public service broadcaster TV 2. The findings show that TV 2's increasingly non-linear television portfolio has a profound impact on the production practices involved in order to meet the public service obligations. The continuity producers and schedulers develop new ways to secure an audience of scale under these conditions. So far three lessons have been learned: (1) the workflow for promoting content and the demands on the qualities of the promotional material has changed; (2) an understanding of the interplay between linear and Subscription-Video-On-Demand (SVOD) scheduling is emerging; and (3) a renewed focus has been put on branding the viewer-provider relationship. The chapter concludes that the production of on-air scheduling for an audience of scale makes the contours of a television paradigm visible in which a distinction between linear and non-linear television does not really apply. Chapter 6 continues the analysis of the production culture from within the television company. The focus is on the problems of scheduling a SVOD service and a linear niche channel for a commercially and politically important young audience segment on a very small national market. The analysis highlights the economic and communicative interdependence between the two platforms and points out three dilemmas influencing the work of the schedulers. The traditional tactics and strategic practices are increasingly being disrupted by SVOD scheduling, yet adapted to an industry that struggles to entangle the logics of the interplay between the linear and the non-linear.

The book concludes in Chapter 7, and it returns to the tensions between the two television paradigms in this introduction and raps up the results and conclusions from the empirical work across Chapters 3–6. It presents fundamental features of a third television paradigm: *digital television* that the current practices of scheduling are producing and elaborates five issues for discussion about the television industry and television as a medium in the digital era: (1) No simple distinctions between a linear and a non-linear television paradigm seem fruitful as a point of departure for empirical studies. (2) A theoretical understanding of television development as technologically driven and linear must be questioned too. (3) The political and cultural contexts in witch television as a medium and the specific companies are embedded are very important, and this will produce differences between the kind of television we experience now and will experience in the future. No fixed or unified development of television can be expected across the television industry even if television is an international phenomenon. (4) Public service television is able to adapt technologically and culturally. It has proven to be very adaptive, flexible and pragmatic throughout television history. Especially in the Nordic countries, companies are very strong institutions with political agency and popular among the audience because of their ability to cater to and stimulate new viewer habits. (5) In the theoretical conceptualisation of television not only change but also continuity and sustainability need to be considered if we want to understand and contribute to a re-formulated television theory for the digital era.

References

Agency of Culture and Palaces (2019) *Mediernes udvikling i Danmark: Internetbrug og enheder.* København: Slots- og Kulturstyrelsen.

Agency of Culture and Palaces (2018) *Mediernes udvikling i Danmark: Streaming af audiovisuelle medier.* København: Slots- og Kulturstyrelsen.

BARB (2019) *The Viewing Report. Our Annual Exploration of the UK's Viewing Habits.* London: BARB.

Brown, N. (1984) The Political Economy of the Television (Super) Text. *Quarterly Review of Film Studies,* 9(3), pp. 174–182.

DR's Public Service Kontrakt 2019–2013. (2018) Kulturministeriet.

Eastman, S. T. and Ferguson, D. A. (2013) (eds.) *Media Programming. Strategies and Practices.* Boston: Wadsworth Cengage Learning.

Eastman, S. T. and Ferguson, D. A. (2009) (eds.) *Media Programming. Strategies & Practices.* Boston: Wadsworth Cengage Learning.

Ellis, J. (2011) Interstitials: How the 'Bits in Between' Define the Programmes. In P. Grainge (ed.) *Ephemeral Media. Transitory Screen Culture from Television to YouTube.* London: Palgrave, pp. 59–69.

Ellis, J. (2000a) *Seeing Things. Television in the Age of Uncertainty.* London: I.B. Tauris Publishers.

Ellis, J. (2000b) Scheduling: The Last Creative Act in Television? *Media, Culture and Society,* 22(1), pp. 25–38.

Ellis, J. (1982) *Visible Fictions.* London: Routledge.

Enli, G. and Syvertsen, T. (2016) The End of Television – Again! How Television Is Still Influenced by Cultural Factors in the Age of Digital Intermediaries. *Media and Communication,* 4(3), pp. 142–153.

European Commission (2019) *Digital Economy and Societal Index Report 2019.* European Commission.

Fiske, J. and Hartley, J. (1978/2003) *Reading Television.* London: Routledge.

Grainge, P. and Johnson, C. (2018) From Catch-Up TV to Online TV: Digital Broadcasting and the Case of BBC iPlayer. *Screen,* 59(1), pp. 21–40.

Gray, J. (2010) *Shows Sold Separately. Promos, Spoilers, and Other Media Paratexts.* New York: New York University Press.

Howard, H. H., Kievman M. S. and Moore, B. A. (1994) *Radio, TV and Cable Programming.* Iowa: Iowa State University Press.

Johnson, C. (2019) *On-line TV.* London: Routledge.

Johnson, C. (2013). The Continuity of 'Continuity': Flow and the Changing Experience of Watching Broadcast Television. *Key Words,* 11, pp. 1–23.

Johnson, C. (2012) *Branding Television.* London: Routledge.

Lotz, A. (2017) *Portals: A Treatise on Internet-Distributed Television.* Ann Arbor: Michigan Publishing.

Lotz, A. (2014) *The Television Will Be Revolutionized.* New York: New York University Press.

Oxvig, M. (2018) "Norden står til at modtage milliardinvesteringer i datacentre", *ITWatch* 20.11. 2018 (Accessed 20-11-2018).

Paterson, R. (1990) A Suitable Schedule for the Family. In A. Goodwin and G. Whannel (eds.) *Understanding Television.* London Routledge, pp. 30–42.

Reddy, S. K., Aronson, J. E. and Stam, A. (1998) SPOT: Scheduling Programs Optimally for Television. *Management Science,* 44(1), pp. 83–102.

Scannell, P. (1996). *Radio, Television and Modern Life.* London: Sage.

Søndergaard, H. (2003) Programfladestyring og organisationsforandringer i nordiske public service-fjernsyn. *Mediekultur,* 35, pp. 5–23.

Søndergaard, H. (1994) *DR i TV-konkurrencens tidsalder.* Frederiksberg: Forlaget Samfundslitteratur.

Stigel, J. (2006) Continuity og tv-reklame. In S. Hjarvard (ed.) *Dansk tv's historie,* Frederiksberg: Samfundslitteratur, pp. 291–330. [Continuity and TV commercials]

Stigel, J. (2004) TV's egenreklame og kanalstemmen. *MedieKultur,* 37, pp. 24–37.

Stigel, J. (2001). Aesthetics of the Moment in Television. In G. Agger and J. F. Jensen (eds.) *The Aesthetics of Television.* Aalborg: Aalborg University Press, pp. 25–52.

Tiedge, J. T. and Ksobiech, K. J. (1987) Counterprogramming Primetime Network Television. *Journal of Broadcasting & Electronic Media,* 31(1), pp. 41–55.

Tiedge, J. T. and Ksobiech, K. J. (1986) The "Lead-In" Strategy for Prime-Time TV: Does It Increase the Audience? *Journal of Communication,* 36(3), pp. 51–63.

Tilladelse til TV 2 Danmark A/S til at udøve public service programvirksomhed 2019–2023. (2018) Kulturministeriet.

Williams, R. (1974) *Television: Technology and Cultural Form.* London: Fontana/Collins.

Ytreberg, E. (2002) Continuity in Environments. The Evolution of Basic Practices and Dilemmas in Nordic Television Scheduling. *European Journal of Communication,* 17(3), pp. 283–304.

2 The schedule as a TV genre
Theoretical approach

Introduction

The schedule is one of the defining features of television as a medium, and it is part of a creative process producing the top level of the television text. It has been produced since the early days of television mirroring and shaping everyday life in different national and regional contexts. As described in Chapter 1 the schedule is much more than distribution of the television programmes. It performs five important *communicative functions*, and it serves as the interface between the viewers and the television company. The three tiers of this televisual texts, (1) the catalogue, (2) the horizontal and vertical structures and time zones, and (3) the on-air broadcast of the schedule including commercials and 'continuity,' have drawn very little academic attention, and it is safe to say that television studies have been strangely indifferent to this part of television. An important reason for the lack of academic interest may be that the schedule is considered an interruption of the proper television text, the programmes, in two ways: the schedule is the carrier of commercial breaks and sponsorship announcements. It is also the carrier of self-promotional material in the shape of the many types of interstitials with a paratextual function to either the upcoming programmes or the television company and its channels and platforms. The two small waves of interest in doing scheduling studies presented in Chapter 1 were connected to important stages in the development of television and its impact on society. The first connected to understanding television as a medium in the 1970s and the second to understand the changes to television industry during the 1980s and 1990 in Europe. In this chapter the emerging third wave of scheduling studies will be presented followed by a presentation of this book's theoretical approach to the schedule and to scheduling.

This approach is based on a specific understanding of genre that has conceptual as well as methodological advantages for understanding television production in an industrial context. Finally, the chapter discusses the interpretation of the medium-viewer relationship and the conceptualisations of the audience embedded in the production of the schedule. The work of the schedulers is extremely dependent on traditional and new sources for gaining knowledge about the audience with the purpose to predict viewing patterns and securing an audience for the companies' channels and services. Thus, the audience is, so to speak, 'in production.' The chapter finally presents and discusses recent research on the impact of personalisation based on algorithms with a special focus on the challenges and possibilities for public service television.

The third wave

During the last ten years a renewed interest in studying the schedule and scheduling has emerged in the light of the present changes to television in the digital era. Important contributions to what I regard as a third wave in scheduling studies question the theoretical understanding, which developed in the pre-digital era, of television as a flow-organised textual phenomenon. Using branding theory, Johnson (2012) provides us with a comprehensive analysis of the efforts made to work the identity of the provider into a single brand with distinctive values in the eyes of the viewers. This is done in the context of intensified competition for attention in the economic and emotional markets. Johnson's study compares the channel branding strategies and campaigns of the BBC, ITV1 and Channel 4 with the American television networks ABC, NBC, CBS and Fox over a 30-year period. As Johnson's findings suggest, it has become increasingly difficult to predict linear viewing patterns. Nevertheless, efforts to attract and hold the attention of the viewers are still paramount, and they have become more important than ever.

In line with Johnson's interest in how the American and British television industries adapts their industrial logic and business models, Ihlebæk et al. (2014) compare how schedulers and promoters of public service and commercial channels in the Norwegian television market revise and renew their 'toolkit' (p. 14) to face these scheduling challenges. Special attention is given to building so-called 'junctions' (ibid., p. 9) in continuity, where the multi-platform provider uses different forms of cross-promotion in order to 'herd' the viewers to stay tuned within its environment of streaming services, websites and main and niche channels. These findings are largely supported by Doyle's analysis of the work of schedulers at MTV UK (2013). These new tools, which aim to support continued viewing on a different platform, are also an obvious difference observed at a textual level by Johnson (2013). In her comparative study of continuity on the BBC on one evening in 1985 and in 2010, the need for spatial metaphors is underpinned by the effort to describe the new temporal structures and the generic changes to the providers' communicative behaviour. These findings are supported by Lassen (2018) in her analysis of how scheduling and cross channel promotion developed in DR from 2005 to 2015. In her comparison of schedules from 2005, 2010 and 2015 Lassen's analysis shows how the amount of 'junctions' has grown during the proliferation of digital channels since 2009 in DR indicating that the public service company is eager to make the many different kinds of content available to the audience (Lassen 2018: 118–123). Furthermore, Lassen argues that to the schedulers 'counter programming' based on genres has become increasingly possible and important within the portfolio and not just as a strategy used in the competition with other companies (ibid.: 129). This is used in order to secure extended choice, and to meet diversity as a public service obligation in the overall portfolio even if the single channel becomes less diverse in terms of genres or subject matter. Lassen's analysis also points out how cross channel promotion included in 'continuity' has grown in the period and with a strong emphasis on the main channel's promotion of immediate or future content available on the niche channels in the portfolio. The niche channels do not cross promote to the main channel DR1, to each other or to the streaming service DRTV (ibid.: 139–141). According to Lassen this is a strange policy that does not take advantage of the possibilities for moving viewers between niche channels or from the niche channels to the mainstream as well as keeping them within the portfolio. In other words, Lassen's analysis shows that in 2015 the main channel is still the 'mothership' in the portfolio addressing a large mainstream audience. This scheduling practice could be viewed as part of DR's efforts to meet the public service obligation to serve as a virtual gathering place for the Danes in small and large communities, which is still an important part of its political legitimacy in the digital era. Similar trajectories seem to guide the use of on-air announcers and channel voices still in place in European public service television as part of identity building and communicating a personalised relationship between the provider and the viewers (Van Den Bulck and Enli 2014b).

As pointed out by Ellis (2011), interstitials and the promotion of the programmes in general are probably getting more important as the number of companies with large portfolios of channels and services is growing. This means that the third tier of the schedule, the on-air schedule, comes into renewed focus, and in many ways the findings in these research contributions underline how on-air scheduling and 'continuity' production have become an increasingly difficult task. On the one hand, it is more important than ever in producing audience ratings and draws on professional knowledge and practises from the linear television paradigm; on the other hand, it may be a task that loses its importance in the shift towards a more non-linear use of television content. As pointed out by Johnson (2019) television and the internet are 'indelibly intertwined' (p. 1), and the future might entail a scenario where non-linear editorially curation based on algorithmic knowledge of user behaviour and preferences is the only way to schedule television. In Chapter 7 of this book I will return to these discussions, and whatever the future, it is safe to say that the communicative functions of the schedule and of 'continuity' are challenged by the need to incorporate the viewers' enhanced choice and content control (Van Den Bulck and Enli 2014a). The understanding of how the schedule and scheduling currently changes in this book is based on a genre approach, and in the following section I will elaborate this theoretical approach and its methodological advantages in doing industry and production studies.

A genre theoretical approach to the schedule

To regard the schedule as a specific televisual genre builds on the five communicative functions it performs in the communicative processes between television and the viewers. This approach may seem a bit controversial as the concept is often used to categorise different types of programmes. However, among the contributors to the first wave of studies into the schedule as a defining feature of television's discourse elaborated in Chapter 1 this approach is in fact argued. John Hartley (1986) points out that the schedule is an autonomous televisual genre with its own specialised production units, conventions and appeals as well as viewer experiences (p. 121). Regarding the schedule as a genre is also argued by Søndergaard (1994: 41) in his attempt to understand the specific aesthetics of the schedule as a televisual discourse. In order to address these textual and sociological aspects the approach to the schedule as a genre in this book builds on a pragmatic understanding of genre. In line with Todorov's understanding of genre (1989, 1990) and in line with the philosophy of language approach to genre suggested by Bakhtin (1952/1986) genre is understood as *language use/parole*. Genre is a phenomenon connected to the conventional aspects as well as the dynamics of language use. The conventional aspects of genres are in this theoretical perspective provisional and of a historical nature, constantly in the loop of being constituted, reproduced in different variations and reshuffled (Neale 1980: 60), which again is producing new conventional aspects. This understanding of genre is based on a pragmatic understanding of what fundamentally characterises human meaning production in everyday life and in professional contexts, in which genre also plays an important role. Genres are compared to the way social norms work structuring human communication and social expectations in specific situations but changeable through the change-producing power of human agency. Furthermore, the approach is based on an understanding that genres have to be analysed in specific historic and contextual circumstances. In short, they are social and historic phenomena.

Positioning genre within the realm of *language use* and within a pragmatic perspective on the norms and conventions of language use makes genre a very messy thing, but never the less extremely important in communication processes. As a consequence, the empirical frame of reference is the *function* of genre and the question of what genre *does* in communicative processes between senders, receivers and textual phenomena. This epistemological understanding of genre also recognises that it is possible to use genre labels in many different ways adding to the messiness of the term. Labels are based on experiences of similarities between groups of texts typically based on theme, semantics, composition, mode of address and use. Nevertheless, there are three problems to this truism. First, *the criteria* of defining a genre as a group of texts with similarities can be changed: for instance semantic criteria or target group criteria can be used. This means that a text can belong to many different genres at the same time. Second, the *level of definition can be changed.* Macro-categories grouping a corpus of texts like entertainment, television fiction or social media can be used as the categorisation tool. But micro-categories of components 'inside' a single text can also be used: for instance epic, didactic and dramatic parts of a text or micro-categories, like entertainment and information, in a text. This also means that a text can belong to many different genres at the same time. Third, genre is used to cover aspects regarding *texts as well as phenomena outside of the text.* Genre is involving expectations held by media users and thus in the interpretation processes of texts, and genre also involves production and distribution categories as well as commercial categories used by the producers of media and the media industry. In short, a strong hermeneutic dimension is to be included in understanding what genre does in communication processes.

All of this makes genre a complex phenomenon not easy to handle. However, for exactly the same reason, genre is an important analytical and methodological concept to use in empirical research into media production. Media production studies are often driven by an ambition to find an approach to media texts and media production with an integrating ability able to answer questions about why changes in the media output happen (Ytreberg 1999; Grindstaff 2002; Jensen 2008; Kjus 2009; Bruun 2011, 2012). The approach is also driven by an interest in understanding the kind of forces and processes involved in these changes (Bruun 2010). A pragmatic genre approach is fruitful as an integrating tool, because it can bypass two classic dichotomies. First, the question of what is driving change? Is change produced by systemic forces, for instance technology, economy and competition, *or* is it the change producing forces of human agency, for instance creativity, artistic vision and imagination? The second classic problem, or dichotomy, is that research *either* gets focussed on texts *or* contexts, but has difficulties in understanding the connection between the two (Ytreberg 2000). The pragmatic approach to genre is able to bridge texts and contexts as well as consider systemic forces and forces of human agency in understanding changes to media output, e.g. the schedule. But the sociological orientation needs to be enhanced. This is needed because within media studies the pragmatic approach to genre is predominantly *a text theory* occupied with different kinds of text and textual developments (Mittell 2001). It is to a much lesser degree a sociological and cognitive theory of genre as a kind of knowledge structuring actions on an individual and social level. If the aim indeed is to understand what genre does in empirical communication processes a stronger focus on human meaning making is needed.

Media texts and contexts

A cognitive approach to understand the connection between audiovisual fiction and emotional processes in the human brain has already been argued in film theory (Bordwell 1985; Grodal 1997). Following this perspective, genre knowledge can be said to have a kind of existence in the human brain and body. Furthermore, an interest in the sociological dimension of genre as a kind of knowledge held by media users and by producers can be found in audience studies and text production studies, respectively. In socio-cognitive audience research an important theoretical inspiration is cognitive psychology and schema theory linked to contemporary brain research in the natural sciences (Shore 1996; Höijer and Werner 1998; Hagen 1998). Genres, understood as schemata, are frameworks for interpreting and organising experiences, expectations and understandings. These genre schemata are not recipes, however, but seen as a sort of frame of reference built by the individual using media products, and used in making sense of new experiences and in reshuffling existing and building new genre schemata. In this approach the genre schema involves the trans-cultural biological conditions of the human brain as well as psychological, sociological and cultural conditions all presumed to influence the production of meaning. Empirical research inspired by this theoretical approach shows that genre schemata do exist as a kind of knowledge held by different audiences, and similarities in genre schemata are found among audiences sharing the same demographics, social and national backgrounds (Höijer 1991, 1996; Bruun 2004). However, as Shore argues (1998: 7), the schema theoretical approach has the potential to be equally fruitful *in media production research*. A socio-cognitive perspective on genre used in the analysis of professional *text production cultures* is convincingly argued: for instance by Berkenkotter and Huckin (1993). Drawing on a reconceptualised rhetorical view on genre from a sociological perspective (Miller 1984), and drawing on philosophy of language and ethnomethodology in the analysis of academic text production, the results point to the benefits of using this approach also when analysing professional media production cultures. Berkenkotter and Huckin strongly emphasise that in a production context genre is to be regarded as a kind of *knowledge* held by and used creatively by the participants of a specific production culture (ibid.: 485). All in all, a stronger sociological orientation is added to the integrating perspective of genre in media production analysis.

But why is this enhancement important? There are three major reasons. First, because production of television, and the majority of professional media production, takes place in organisational and industrial context marked by economic, political and technological aspects on different levels. Individuals work together in these specific contexts producing different kinds of texts that are in very different ways dependent on the creative power of human agency. Second, the enhancement is important because the agents in these organisations are trained professional media producers with an expert knowledge, and with a power over the actual products being produced, distributed and sold. And third, because we are dealing with text producing practises performed by professionals. These practises can be hard to put into words by the professionals because they are part of professional training processes. Sometimes they are only visible in actual actions and part of what Polanyi calls the 'tacit dimension' of knowledge (Polanyi 1967).

Methodological advantages

In the following section of the Chapter I argue that there are three major advantages of applying a genre approach in media production studies, and these are connected to the methodological design of the empirical investigation as well as to the production of findings.

Knowledge producing integration

A genre approach is able to integrate the texts produced in the methodological design of a media production study. This is very helpful, and I will return to elaborate on the reason for this advantage below. However, it is important to acknowledge that a genre approach is not just a methodological tool. It has an integrating perspective that is producing knowledge as well, and therefore not just a tool. The approach has a very big say in *getting access* to construct an analytical object. Getting access is no doubt the biggest obstacle to production studies. The media are professional organisations and businesses and part of the social sphere. They form a competitive system between private commercial businesses and a dual system of commercial and public service organisations. As a rule, the researcher does not have access to do research within these organisations, but is hopefully given access either as a gift or as a trade of services between the researcher and the media organisation. In order to get access, however, the professionals inside these media organisations have to be interested in helping the researcher. Taking the products produced in television by these professionals as the point of departure asking for their help to understand why the products turn out as they do, is very productive. That is because the approach entails a high degree of compatibility. It *positions* the interviewees as professional individuals with power, and not just as 'puppets on a string.' This is also compatible with their own self-image, not different from other professionals working in the creative industries (Bruun 2016). Furthermore, a genre approach is also compatible with the way these professionals think of their own profession and what could be called their *professional knowledge*. Television producers think and talk in terms of genre, in genre differences and in audiences for different genres. They think and talk in terms of professional and creative competences connected to genres as well. And finally, taking this into account makes the researcher seem as an almost sensible person to help. In this study the genre approach to the schedule and to scheduling as a professional practise helped getting access because the many professionals involved in producing the schedule are overlooked when it comes to understanding television and the creative processes behind its content, even if they do certainly not belong to staff 'below the line' in the television industry (Caldwell 2008). My interests in their work gave me extended access to do observations and to interviews, and I was met with a genuine effort to introduce the academic to the production processes and the culture involved.[1] This was indeed needed because the existing literature on the issue of scheduling is very sparse. Furthermore, the timing of the study also played a big role in getting extended access. As I have elaborated elsewhere television studies and the television industry currently share an interest in issues and questions about the future of television (Bruun and Frandsen 2017).

The preoccupation with genre in television production is really not surprising and very much a result of the *pervasive use of genre* in the whole industry. This is trivial and easy to take for granted, nevertheless important to consider. First of all, the products, e.g. channels, websites or programmes, are labelled and scheduled according to genres able to attract the right audience in order to meet strategic goals. This rather traditional approach is also used by the streaming companies in the ways that they present their products, e.g. Netflix, as demonstrated by Lobato's analysis of the company's catalogue (2018). Second, *the television companies as physical organisations* are structured according to the production of genres: for instance divisions or units of news, fiction, entertainment, lifestyle, etc. Furthermore, these companies are staffed to facilitate the production of specific genres: for instance schedulers, on-air promotion producers, commissioning editors of entertainment, fiction and documentaries. And finally, in dealing with in-house and out-sourced productions genres are very important categorisation tools. Third, *the political regulation and legal control systems of the media* and indeed television on a national and international level are also using genres, for instance, when formulating remits for public service media, and regulating the conditions for commercial media. Finally, *the television industry as an international business* is very much a trade where the products are organised in different genre categories: for instance the international trade with programmes and formats at MIPCom and on international fairs and festivals. The production companies used by the broadcasters are often specialised in the production of specific genres, and the knowledge in the kind of theory generated by the television industry itself is based on genres: for instance rapports on quality and 'how-do-to –X'-books and production guidelines are taking genres as a point of departure. Given the ubiquitous status of genre in the industry the genre approach gives the researcher an opportunity to use the actual corpus of texts produced actively in gathering data. This has played an important role in my study of scheduling. I produced comprehensive catalogues of how the on-air schedule was structured, as well as the use of cross-promotion and identity branding during selected weeks in 2014 and 2016. These catalogues serve as the analytical object in Chapters 3 and 4 but were also used during the interviews.[2] It turned out to be a very productive tool. It produced a *factual reference* for talking about the rather ephemeral communicative features of the schedule and its production and it was *helping memory* along by grounding it in descriptions of specific examples and processes and not just opinions. It produced *a sense of the cultural contributions* made by the professional interviewees and they all really liked browsing through it. Finally, it *validated* my work, because the interviewees added information and reflections. Apart from these methodological advantages, the integrating abilities of the genre approach are also producing findings. First of all, the scheduling study supports the theoretical argument that producing media products involves interpretation of a pre-existing genre tradition as a corpus of texts within a specific television company and within a specific historical context. Second, this entails communicative intentionality, regarding the communicative purpose of the genre and its intended audience. All in all, the results of the study really support Joli Jensen's suggestion that cultural production is to be regarded as interpretation, and therefore production research needs to combine theoretical approaches from both sociology and the humanities (Jensen 1984). Using a genre approach is one fruitful way to do this. Furthermore, the notion that genre is part of conventionalised yet dynamic language use in a specific context is also supported very strongly. To sum up on this first advantage of knowledge production, using a genre approach supports a double role of the interviewees: they serve as informants as well as representatives of the values and 'belief systems' (Caldwell 2008) of the production culture that has undergone important changes in its understanding of the purpose of producing a specific kind of content and the intended audience.

Texts cum contexts

The second major advantage of a genre approach is its ability to highlight the *interaction* between the cultural products: the texts, and the organisational and industrial contexts. In fact, the texts are interwoven with contextual factors in such a way that it is rather difficult to draw a line between the two. Factors like the normative status of a genre, the models for recruitment of new talent within specific production cultures as well as the distribution of editorial and economic power within the media company are part of the products produced. Furthermore, factors like the strategic use of certain genres by media companies in order to, for instance, fulfil the public service remit and move public service to non-linear distribution platforms influence the products. Finally, and very importantly economics influences the products in a very concrete way. All in all, this multitude of concurrent contextual factors of the television business must be considered in the effort to understand changes.

Professional genre knowledge

A third major advantage of a genre approach in production studies is that it provides an empirical access to the professional genre knowledge involved in the different fields or 'biotopes' of media production. I have already touched upon this advantage in connection with the two methodological advantages described, but I would like to add some more to this regarding the *different kinds of professional knowledge* a genre approach is able to elicit. In television production I would suggest that professional genre knowledge is embedded in *specific* conventionalised practises within a larger media production environment. A genre approach is able to frame verbal narratives, actions and practises, and by so doing it is able to gain insight into the *tacit dimension* of media production, that is, gain insight into the conventionalised professional genre knowledge sometimes hard to put in to words. I would also suggest that professional genre knowledge *structures specific commissioning and selection criteria* within a larger editorial system, criteria that can be more or less explicit. Finally, I will suggest that *professional genre knowledge is embedded in relative autonomous production cultures* within an overarching production system that can be driven by public service obligations or commercial logics, or a mixture of both. In this way the production culture of scheduling may differ fundamentally from the one governing the production of news. To sum up, this third advantage of a genre approach points to these three major features of the professional genre knowledge intrinsic to a production culture and its development in a specific social and historic context. These insights are very fruitful because they might help the researcher in understanding the characteristics of media production in specific fields and prevent the researcher from making sweeping generalisations from one production culture to another.

Even if genre is a difficult phenomenon and perhaps even a bit controversial to regard the schedule as a televisual genre, it is a very valuable concept in researching media text production because it contains an integrating perspective that works methodologically as well as analytically. The approach has the ability to highlight the interplay between human agency and different kinds of structural forces involved in specific professional media production cultures. Furthermore, it has the potential to integrate media texts and especially the micro- and meso-levels of production, and by doing so making an empirically grounded contribution to understand why media output change. This empirical grounding may also finally support the macro level of genre analysis. As argued by Mittell (2001: 18–19) the approach enables a cultural politics of genre perspective 'situating genre within power relations' (ibid.:19).

Knowing the audience in scheduling

Intrinsic to the more or less tacit genre knowledge of the producers is a conceptualisation of the audience, and in the process of producing a schedule, the tensions between the two television paradigms are upsetting some of the traditional sources of knowledge. Constructions of this audience in scheduling are based on different sources, which provide formal as well as informal knowledge of the audience. As Ang points out (1991:19), these sources of knowledge about the audience are used within the media organisations to reduce the risk of producing mass communication like television. To 'make an audience' is the fundamental task in television production, because without an audience the economic viability and cultural legitimacy of television disappear. Nevertheless, the audience is 'the ultimate insecurity factor because in principle there is no way to know in advance whether the audience will tune in and stay tuned' (ibid.: 18). As argued by Ettema and Whitney (1994), 'the audience' is then a construction constituted by a range of complex organisational processes of what is regarded as 'institutionally effective audiences that have social meaning and/ or economic value within the system' (1994: 5). These effective audiences include what Ettema and Whitney term the *measured audiences*. At present, this kind of institutional knowledge is constructed by the statistical sample data generated by tools like Kantar Gallup's 'TV Viewing' or other tools from the audience measurement companies like Nielsen in the United States and 100 other countries, or BARB, a partner to Kantar, in the United Kingdom. These data are the imperfect 'hard currency' of the television industry in terms of selling advertisement 'space' in the on-air schedule, for positioning programmes and different forms of promotional campaigns, and it has a huge influence on commissioning and production decisions within the companies (Webster 2014). As a consequence of the growing inaccuracy of the old TV-Meter-survey method, in 2017 the major television companies in the Danish industry agreed to collectively finance a new way of measuring television viewing that includes seven days of streaming the broadcasted content. Even if the validity of the 'currency' has improved, the use of streamed content before linear broadcasting and seven days after is not included, and neither is the use of streaming of content from subscription-financed companies, like Netflix, or social media, like YouTube and Facebook. In short, the audience data produced does not cover all use of audio-visual material in the population, and it does not cover two of the three types of companies that Johnson terms 'online TV' either (2019). To improve this kind of knowledge of the audience other quantitative tools are being used by the individual television companies in order to measure the user patterns and performance of the content on company streaming services, on company apps, on company websites and on social media (Falkenberg Andersen and Jul Hansen 2018: 46–52).

The notion of the institutionally effective audience also includes what Ettema and Whitney call *specialised and segmented audiences*. This kind of knowledge consists of, for example, target group information from lifestyle typologies, based on cluster analysis of values, and research into patterns of viewing behaviour and content choices. This kind of statistical sample-based data is included in the present 'TV Viewing'-measurement in the Danish television industry described above, and this kind of data is widely used to segment the audience into special target groups for the different time slots and channels in the portfolios (Bruun 2014). Data from qualitative methods like focus group pre-tests or post-broadcast evaluations of programmes are also a source of knowledge included. Finally, the notion of 'effective audiences' includes what Ettema and Whitney term the *hypothesised audiences,* which covers the presumed interests and needs of the audience protected by national and international regulations of television, for example protection of children and minorities and/ or the cultural-political obligations of public service media (PSM), e.g. placing shows not considered a good fit for young children in late night time slots (Webster and Phalen 1994). In public service television placing genres considered important to the public service remit in time slot where the audience is available is an example of how this conceptualisation of the audience works.

In addition to these different kinds of formal sources of knowledge, the professional knowledge of the audience held by producers is very important. This kind of knowledge circulates in certain discursive practices, for example in pitching ideas for future channel branding campaigns, in informal conversations and at editorial as well as board meetings (see Bruun 2011, 2014). Espinosa (1982) calls this kind of knowledge of the audience the 'cultural category' (ibid.: 85). The audience is, in this sense, embedded in the television products, because the whole production process behind the final product is informed by this kind of professional knowledge held by individuals and the specific production culture. The importance of the audience conceptualised as a cultural category is probably very much connected to Donald Schön's concept of knowledge-in-action and on the concept of the tacit dimension of knowledge (Polanyi 1967). This means that the notion of the audience is not easily expressed in words, but nevertheless permeates the production process and the final products, in this book the on-air schedule.

The different kinds of knowledge described above are a very important part of the work of the schedulers and continuity producers as Chapters 5 and 6 will show. These multiple sources of knowledge about the audience can give rise to different and even conflicting audience-in-production models at work in scheduling for multi-channel and multi-platform television. As I have argued elsewhere there is a multitude of audience-in-production models at work in television production often associated with different genres and the normative status of these genres (Bruun 2014). In the production of the schedule for public service television these different models are all at work across mainstream channels, niche channels, mono-generic channels and different on-demand services included in the portfolios. The development in public service television in Europe after the period of single channel television monopolies has been marked by the efforts to do socio-cultural segmentation by taste and interests in order to meet the public service obligations within a competitive television market. This means that 'the audience' is by no means neither a homogenous nor a stable entity but a dynamic phenomenon that has to be interpreted and re-interpreted continuously in the context of developments in the industry. For example, specific target groups among the potential audience might be of greater value than others for economic and/or political reasons: for example attracting a young audience; the placing of certain genres associated with specific organisational needs may give priority to one audience-in-production model over others, for example the news cast.

Personalisation

The conceptualisations of the audience based on these sources of knowledge in the industry are still very much based on the linear television paradigm. As described by Johnson (2019) the television industries in many countries are trying to improve what is termed this traditional 'exposure model' (p. 137) of making viewer behaviour translate into commodities as well as cultural-political legitimation. Currently, the possibility of harvesting data based on access to detailed and nuanced information about user behaviour on non-linear services included in the portfolios is being added to the sources of knowledge. This new kind of knowledge is being included in the scheduling practises of the television companies. An example is the internal data on the number of subscribers on the company's streaming service, and the number of views of content and the time spend on the service, which can be used to promote the service publicly. Mads Møller Tommerup Andersen documents how DR uses data from its streaming service to promote specific cultural-political aspects of DR3's content catalogue, like the amount of views of the Danish-language factual series even if the TV ratings show a different story. Like BBC3, DR3 is going to be an online only service in 2020 (Andersen 2018). However, the framework of the established knowledge sources about the audience in the companies plays an important role in understanding this new kind of knowledge available because 'big data' come with a lot of problems and it is not in any way a simple mirror of what content individual viewers like or would like to have more of in the future (Webster 2014). Algorithms are used to turn big data in to operational tools with the purpose to predict the collective user patterns and to do recommendation relevant to the available audience. According to Johnson (2019) *collaborative filtering* is a form of machine learning used by online television services to generate predictions and recommendations: '[They] operate by tracking and recording the behaviour of individual users and comparing it with others who display similar behaviours (...) in order to identify patterns of media use' (p. 143). Johnson describes the understanding of human behaviour in this approach to cultural choices as relatively reduction-istic. It reduces human behaviour to mathematical processes (p. 145). Nevertheless, this source for knowledge of the audience has a cultural impact just like the more traditional sources to gain knowledge of the audience in the television industry in order to reduce the risks of mass communication. In this way, collaborative filtering algorithms are not neutral and separate from human agency (Sandvig et al. 2016). Algo-rithms are programmed by humans and they are based on data pro-duced by human behavior, and in this sense algorithms are producing culture, as Hallinan and Striphas argue (2016). The question is, how-ever, if and how collaborative filtering algorithms based directly on user behaviour will change basic conceptualisations of the audience in the industry and perhaps make the other sources of knowledge less important commercially as well as cultural-politically? And how does the production culture of professional schedulers and continuity pro-ducers navigate between the sophisticated audience data based on statistics and on qualitative findings from audience studies and the new sources based on algorithmic predictions of user behaviour and recommendations of content? Especially for public service television companies this has the potential to upset the fundamental normative ideal of producing a mixed schedule in linear television in order to meet the core public service obligations of information, enlighten-ment and entertainment accessible to all citizens. Embedded in this normative ideal of universality is a conceptualisation of the audience, which is of course an ideal and, in reality, already compromised by decades of target group strategies, multi-channel portfolios fragment-ing the audience, niche channels for special taste segment and fierce competition in the television ecosystem. The dystopian scenario for such an ideal is, however, the mono-generic viewer indifferent to the mixed diet of genres and subject areas of the linear schedule and only interested in consuming e.g. American fiction. In such a scenario the recursive data flows will make viewer choice into a 'hall of mirrors' as pointed out by Bennett (2018: 115), and public service will no longer be able to meet its obligations to a democratic society by supporting an informed citizenry. A common solution to this challenge repre-sented by the non-linear television paradigm is to call for the deve-lopment of a 'public service algorithm' in order to counter balance the possible ideological pitfalls of personalisation in the companies (Moe and Van den Bulck 2018: 16). Hallvard Moe and Hilde Van den

Bulck (2018) map the level of personalisation implemented and the attitude towards it in European public service television companies. The findings show that the majority of the public service companies investigated are positive towards securing universality through personalisation. It is perceived as a way to secure and enhance individual relevance of the public service experience and to support an element of serendipity. Nevertheless, a number of concerns are also present, e.g. binge viewing instead of a mix of genres, the protection of privacy against the advantage of using a personal log-in and the need for a high level of privacy protection in general in order to ensure the audience's trust. All in all, these companies seem ripe with dilemmas when faced with this new opportunity for personalisation based on big data even if some of the companies are less concerned than others. As the book will illuminate the schedule and its production are marked by similar challenges and dilemmas, especially when the public service company is financed not by a licence fee or a tax but on commercials and subscription.

Notes

1 In Chapters 5 and 6 I will elaborate on the concrete design of the production study.
2 In Chapters 3 and 4 I elaborate in more detail on the specific methodological design of the analysis of the schedules.

References

Andersen, M. M. T. (2018) DR3 på flow og streaming – en todelt kanalanalyse. *MedieKultur*, 65, pp. 138–157.

Ang, I. (1991) *Desperately Seeking the Audience*. London: Routledge.

Bakhtin, M. M. (1952/1987) 'The Problem of Speech Genres. In C. Emerson & M. Holquist (eds.) *Speech Genres & Other Late Essays*. Austin: University of Texas Press, pp. 60–102.

Bennett, J. (2018) Public Service Algorithms. In D. Freedman and V. Gabolt (eds.) *A Future for Public Service Television*. London: Goldsmiths Press, pp. 11–121.

Berkenkotter, C. and Huckin, T. N. (1993) Rethinking Genre from a Socio-cognitive Perspective. *Written Communication*, 10(4), pp. 475–509.

Bordwell, D. (1985) *Narration in the Fiction Film*. London: Methuen.

Bruun, H. (2016) *The Qualitative Interview in Media Production Studies*. In C. Paterson, D. Lee, A. Saha and A. Zoellner (eds.) *Advancing Media Production Research. Shifting Sites, Methods, and Politics*. Basingstoke: Palgrave Macmillan, pp. 131–147.

Bruun, H. (2014) Conceptualizing the Audience in Political Talk Show Production. *European Journal of Communication*, 29(1), pp. 3–16.

Bruun, H. (2012) Changing Production Culture in Television Satire. *Northern Lights*, 10, pp. 41–56.

Bruun, H. (2011) *Dansk tv-satire. Underholdning med kant.* Copenhagen: Books on Demand.

Bruun, H. (2010) Genre and Interpretation in Production: A Theoretical Approach. *Media, Culture and Society*, 32(5), pp. 723–737.

Bruun, H. (2004) *Daytime Talkshows i Danmark.* Aarhus: Modtryk.

Bruun, H. and Frandsen, K. (2017) Tid og Timing – et metodisk perspektiv på produktionsanalyse. *MedieKultur*, 62, pp. 119–133.

Caldwell, J. T. (2008) *Production Culture. Industrial Reflexivity and Critical Practices in Film and Television.* Durham: Duke University Press.

Doyle, G. (2013) Innovation in the Use of Digital Infrastructures. TV Scheduling Strategies and Reflections on Public Policy. In T. Storsul and A. Krumsvik (eds.) *Media Innovations. A Multidisciplinary Study of Change.* Göteborg: Nordicom, pp. 111–125.

Ellis, J. (2011). Interstitials: How the 'Bits in Between' Define the Programmes. In P. Grainge (ed.) *Ephemeral Media. Transitory Screen Culture from Television to YouTube.* London: Palgrave, pp. 59–69.

Ettema, J. S. and Whitney, D. C. (1994) *Audiencemaking: How the Media Create the Audience.* London: Sage.

Espinosa, P. (1982) The Audience in the Text: Ethnographic Observations of a Hollywood Story Conference. *Media, Culture & Society*, 4(1), pp. 77–86.

Falkenberg Andersen, S. and Jul Hansen, M. (2018) *Brandbog 2018 – viden til indsigt.* In-house document. Odense: TV 2 Analyse.

Grindstaff, L. (2002) *The Money Shot: Trash, Class, and the Making of TV Talk Shows.* Chicago: University of Chicago Press.

Grodal, T. (1997) *Moving Pictures. A New Theory of Film Genres, Feelings, and Cognition.* Oxford: Clarendon Press.

Hagen, I. (1998) Creation of Socio-Cultural Meaning. In B. Höijer and A. Werner (eds.) *Cultural Cognition. New Perspectives in Audience Theory.* Göteborg: Nordicom, pp. 59–72.

Hallinan, B. and Striphas, T. (2016) Recommended For You: The Netflix Prize and the Production of Algorithmic Culture. *New Media and Society*, 18(1), pp. 117–137.

Hartley, J. (1986) Out of Bounds: The Myth of Marginality. In L. Masterman (ed.) *Television Mythologies. Stars, Shows and Signs.* London: Comedia Publishing/MK Media Press, pp. 118–127.

Höijer, B. (1996) *Audiences' Expectations on the Interpretations of Different Television Genres: A Socio-cognitive Approach.* Paper IAMCR-conference, Sydney.

Höijer, B. (1991) *Lustfylld glömska, kreativ illusion och realitetsprövning. Om publikens tankeprocesser vid tittande på fiction och fakta.* Stockholm: Sverige Radio, 15.

Höijer, B. and Werner, A. (1998) (eds.) *Cultural Cognition. New Perspectives in Audience Theory.* Göteborg: Nordicom.

Ihlebæk, K., Syvertsen, T. and Ytreberg, E. (2014). Keeping Them and Moving Them: TV Scheduling in the Phase of Channel and Platform Proliferation. *Television & New Media*, 15(5), pp. 470–486.

Jensen, J. (1984) An Interpretive Approach to Culture Production. In W. D. Rowland & B. Watkins (eds.) *Interpreting Television: Current Research Perspectives.* London: Sage, pp. 98–118.

Jensen, P.M. (2008) The International Extent and Elasticity of Lifestyle Television. *MedieKultur*, 45, pp. 37–50.

Johnson, C. (2019) *Online TV.* London: Routledge.

Johnson, C. (2013). The Continuity of 'Continuity': Flow and the Changing Experience of Watching Broadcast Television. *Key Words*, 11, pp. 1–23.

Johnson, C. (2012). *Branding Television.* London: Routledge.

Kjus, Y. (2009) *Event Media: Television Production Crossing Media Bounderies.* Ph.d.afhandling, University of Oslo, Norway.

Lassen, J. M. (2018) *DRs tv-virksomhed i forandring: programflade, portefølje og platforme.* PhD thesis, University of Copenhagen.

Lobato, R. (2018) Rethinking International TV Flows Research in the Age of Netflix. *Television and New Media*, 19(3), pp. 241–256.

Miller, C. R. (1984) 'Genre as Social Action,' *Quarterly Journal of Speech*, 70(2), pp. 151–167.

Mittell, J. (2001) A Cultural Approach to Television Genre Theory. *Cinema Journal*, 40(3), pp. 3–24.

Moe, H. and Van den Bulck, H. (2018) Public Service, Universality and Personalization through Algorithms: Mapping Strategies and Exploring Dilemmas. *Media, Culture and Society*, 40(6), pp. 875–892.

Neale, S. (1980) *Genre.* London: British Film Institute.

Polanyi, M. (1967) *The Tacit Dimension.* London: Routledge & Kegan Paul.

Sandvig, C., Hamilton, K., Karahalios, K. and Langbort, C. (2016) When the Algorithm Itself is a Racist: Diagnosing Ethical Harm in the Basic Components of Software. *International Journal of Communication*, 10, pp. 4972–4990.

Shore, B. (1998) Model Theory a Framework for Media Studies. In B. Höijer and A. Werner (eds.) *Cultural Cognition. New Perspectives in Audience Theory.* Göteborg: Nordicom, pp. 41–59.

Shore, B. (1996) *Culture in Mind. Cognition, Culture, and the Problem of Meaning.* Oxford: Oxford University Press.

Søndergaard, H. (1994). *DR i TV-konkurrencens tidsalder.* Frederiksberg: Forlaget Samfundslitteratur.

Todorov, T. (1990) *Genres in Discourse.* Cambridge: Cambridge University Press.

Todorov, T. (1989) *Den fantastiske litteratur.* København: Klim.

Van den Bulck, H. and Enli, G. S. (2014a). Flow Under Pressure: Television Scheduling and Continuity Techniques as Victims of Media Convergence? *Television and New Media*, 15(5), pp. 441–452.

Van den Bulck, H. and Enli, G. S. (2014b). Bye, Bye "Hello Ladies?": In-Vision Announcers as Continuity Technique in a European Postlinear Television Landscape: The Case of Flanders and Norway. *Television and New Media*, 15(5), pp. 453–469.

Webster, J. G. (2014) *The Marketplace for Attention*. Cambridge: The MIT Press.

Webster, J. G. and Phalen, P. F. (1994) Victims, Consumers, or Commodity? Audience Models in Communications Policy. In J. S. Ettema and D. C. Whitney (eds.) *Audiencemaking: How the Media Create the Audience*. London: Sage, pp. 19–37.

Ytreberg, E. (2000) Notes on Text Production as a Field of Inquiry in Media Studies. *Nordicom Review*, 21, pp. 53–62.

Ytreberg, E. (1999) *Allmennkringkastingens autoritet. Endringer i NRK Fjernsynets tekstproduktion 1987–1994*. Oslo: Universitetet i Oslo.

3 Communicative characteristics of the on-air schedule

Introduction

Chapter 2 of this book gave an account of how a renewed interest in scheduling and 'continuity' studies is emerging in television studies in the light of the present changes to television in the digital era. This chapter contributes to this body of research and highlights and discusses the changing communicative behaviour in the on-air schedule with a specific focus on the kind of 'continuity' produced by public service television. Based on a case study of the main channels of the public service companies DR (Danmarks Radio) and TV 2 in Denmark, the chapter suggests that an increasing *divergence* marks the development in the digital era between these two companies. Three major differences are found in the efforts to first retain and 'herd' the viewers within the scope of products (Caldwell 2003), adding a spatial dimension to scheduling. Promoting content available on the non-linear services is produced in continuation of scheduling strategies applied to a multi-channel portfolio but in two different ways. Second, differences are found in the efforts to strengthen the provider-viewer relationship, and third, to stand out with a distinct set of company values. The findings can be regarded as a consequence of the challenges and opportunities facing these companies in terms of funding and in terms of meeting public service obligations navigating the tension between a linear and a non-linear television paradigm.

The two companies are far in cultivating digital television, and they both stimulate new ways of using the medium and the television content among the Danes. To give priority to these transformations is an explicit part of the public service obligation for both companies. In DR's current public service contract with the government (*DR's public service-kontrakt 2019–2023*), the obligation is to address the increase in digital distribution of the content by converting two out of six linear channels to the streaming service during 2020. Furthermore,

DR2 and DRK will be merged and DR will offer only three linear channels by 2020. In TV 2's public service authorisation agreement it is emphasised that access to the main content of channel with public service obligations must be included in the streaming service (*Public service tilladelse TV 2 2019–2023*). In many ways the push towards a non-linear television paradigm is part of the Danish cultural-political ambition in the public service media policy, and not just a survival strategy for the individual companies. Furthermore, both companies are part of a long tradition for cultural-political regulations of the television industry with a focus to protect and stimulate Danish-language television production about Danish society and culture in all genres and subject areas on a national media market with only 5.6 million inhabitants. The two companies have very different funding models and organisational structures. DR is a public provider of radio and television that is 100 per cent funded by a public service tax introduced in 2019. Presently, it offers six linear television channels the streaming service DRTV and the website dr.dk. All of DR's activities are part of the public service obligation, and access to the content regardless of platform is given priority as a result of the Danish public service regulations. A mixture of subscriptions and advertisements funds TV 2, and TV 2 only provides television. Furthermore, TV 2/Danmark is a limited company, entirely owned by the Danish state. It has two divisions. The first is a public service division that includes the main channel, TV 2, and the main channel has scheduled 'windows' for the eight regional news providers that are supported by the public service tax. Second, TV 2/Danmark has a large commercial division, TV 2 Networks, which is completely financed by subscriptions and advertisements, *and has no public service obligations*. This division includes the website, tv2.dk, five niche channels and the streaming service, TV 2 Play. Danish law allows commercial breaks only *between* what are considered 'programmes' or in 'natural breaks' within programmes: for example at half time in a football match.

The scope of public service obligations put to DR and TV 2, respectively, differs, and the obligations for DR are far more detailed and regulated by a detailed four-year contract based on the four-year media agreement between the sitting government and its supporting parties in the parliament. The explicit aim for DR is to emphasises DR's obligation to organise a service for all Danes around four goals or pillars: first, to strengthen the democratic capacity of the citizens; second, to unite Danes in communities both small and large as well as to mirror the diversity of Danish society; third, to stimulate Danish culture and language as well as the Christian cultural heritage;

and finally, to promote knowledge and insight. In addition, the idea of platform neutrality informs the current contract, giving DR 'the right and the obligation to offer public service content on all relevant platforms' (*DR's public service-kontrakt 2019–2023*: 2). This means content has to be universally accessible to all citizens. If, for example, young adults use a tablet or a smartphone, and social network media instead of television, DR's content should – at least in principle – be made accessible on all these platforms and media (Bruun 2018). For both DR and TV 2 the obligation to produce Danish drama is underpinned by hourly quotas, and both have to account for their public serve activities on a yearly basis.

These differences and similarities between the two companies have an impact on the genre characteristics and current developments of the communicative behaviour in the on-air schedule and, as a consequence, on *the kind* of interface produced. The comparative analysis is based on the continuity sequences from DR1 and TV 2 from 9 to 15 November 2014 between 6 and 12 pm. Even if the sample is relatively old the three trends presented below are still accurate at the time of writing, and even if the industrial discourse is that television is changing very fast a lot of things actually stay the same or change rather slowly. Furthermore, the findings regarding the use of cross promotion at DR1 are supported by Lassen's analysis of DR's continuity comparing a week in 2005, 2010 and 2015 (Lassen 2018) as well as the sample from 2016 used in Chapter 4 of this book. Finally, being a bit behind the latest examples and adjustments from the industry is the conditions of time-consuming empirical work. Constructing an analytical object needed for the kind of analysis presented in this chapter and in Chapter 4 of this book is indeed time consuming: the textual catalogue of the continuity sequences needed to do the quantitative and qualitative analysis has to be deduced from the piles of DVDs containing the on-air schedule in its totality. There is no useable metadata available of this part of the televisual text in the media collections at the Danish Royal Library or in Kantar Gallup's database of television viewing in Denmark. As pointed out by Johnson in her book on branding television (2012: 120) these difficulties and time issues are probably one of the reasons for the limited interest in doing this kind of research in television studies.

Trend 1: 'crossroads,' 'roundabouts' or 'one-way streets'

As documented by Ihlebæk et al. (2014) in their analysis of the relationship between Norwegian public service company NRK's main channel NRK1 and its niche channels, DR1 serves, in terms of programming, as a kind of 'mother ship' in the fleet of channels and non-linear services provided by DR. This means that continuity is marked by a high frequency of information pushing the viewers to other DR channels and/ or platforms, in the present or in the near future. These, which I term 'crossroads,' are placed at the intersection between programmes with a potentially strong change in content and/or target group appeal. An example of these frequent 'crossroads' is found at DR1 12 November 2014 at 19:58, directing the viewers to an alternative choice.

An alternative to *Vanens Magt* ['The Power of Habit'], an everyday-life, problem-solving and host-driven factual series, is an episode of a factual, investigative critical series on DR2 (Figure 3.1):

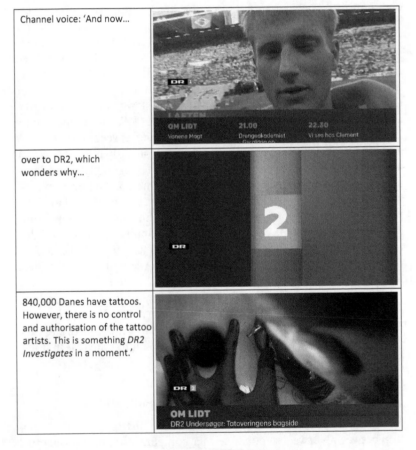

Figure 3.1 Crossroads.

This is basically a choice between two different kinds of television journalism. All the continuity sequences in the material from DR1's prime time schedule contain 'crossroads' for an immediate, alternative choice. In many ways, this is an internal form of counter-programming tactic, which is also used between competing providers. However, 'herding' is used to avoid losing viewers, even if it might split the mother ship's 'herd.' In addition to this very frequently used tactic, DR1 uses what I would like to call 'roundabouts,' in specific time zones of the schedule, with the same purpose as the 'crossroads.' An example of a 'roundabout' would be the one aired on 9 November after the Sunday fiction series at 8 pm, which has a very high expected share of viewers, and before the special Sunday newscast at 9 pm, which normally also has a high share of viewers (Figure 3.2):

Channel voice: 'Before *21Søndag* [the special Sunday evening newscast] in a few moments, we just need to have a look at what is happening on our other channels. DR2 offers satire in the shape of *Nyt fra Jylland* ['News from Jutland'], and

Over at DR3, years of contention between the detectives Hart and Cohle end, in the serial *True Detective*. And

Figure 3.2 Roundabout.

Over at DRK, you can catch a documentary by Anders Østergaard, about the fall of the Berlin Wall.
This is all happening right now.

Here at our place, Kim Bildsøe Lassen [the anchor's name] is standing by with more details on the OWBunker scandal. Here is *21Søndag.'*

Figure 3.2 (Continued).

The temporal structure of the 'roundabouts' has the obvious function of 'herding' the intended viewer to switch channel or platform if something more interesting is on offer somewhere else within the portfolio (linear or non-linear). The other function is to brand DR as a provider with an abundance of content on offer for all its viewers to choose from, and to show that DR has the surplus energy to help the viewers to find what they want. It communicates a conceptualisation of the intended viewers as a heterogeneous group with varied tastes and interests, and finally, it communicates diverse content and universal access as core values of public service media (PSM).

The use of 'crossroads' at TV 2 is very different. In the sample from 2014, only six examples of 'crossroads' to other channels were found, three directing viewers to TV 2/Fri, two to TV 2/Zulu and one to TV 2/

Credits, *Badehotellet* ['The beach hotel'] and 'crossroads' to TV 2 Play	
Credits, schedule outline, trailer for *Avatar* and channel voice: 'We will be ready with a brand new weather forecast in a moment. And after that, you can join the journey to the moon, Pandora… [trailer takes over full screen]	
You will see James Cameron's blockbuster film *Avatar* just after *Vejret* [the weather report].'	

Figure 3.3 Split-screen strategy.

Charlie. However, 'crossroads' that direct the viewers to the streaming service, TV 2 Play, using a banner in the top right-hand corner of the screen (see Figure 3.3), or opportunities to chat on the website tv2.dk with participants in the programme just shown, are also used. In the sample, this happens twice on the Sunday (9 November), and on the Wednesday (12 November). The 'crossroads' offer viewers the option to view more episodes of drama and documentaries produced by TV 2; to chat with the scriptwriter of the crime series *Dicte*; and, on the Wednesday, to chat with the participants in the documentary *Children of Sperm Donors*. 'Roundabouts' are, however, used only once. In this way, TV 2 stands out as a kind of 'one-way street,' trying to make the audience stay tuned to the main channel. It may leave a much more traditional impression of a stand-alone television channel addressing an intended audience, conceptualised as a homogeneous group with a limited choice.[1]

The reasons for the difference between TV 2 and DR1 are, first and foremost, connected to the business model and the organisational split of TV 2/Danmark (between a public service division and a commercial division), and because of the legal framework for TV 2/Danmark. Cross-promotion is allowed between the products produced, because, according to Danish legislation, this is not considered to be advertisement. However, the main channel, TV 2, has to generate a reach in the population so that it can keep up its viability as a commercial channel with public service obligations. The advertisements are sold in bundles *across* the channels in the portfolio, and are priced accordingly. It is crucial to maintain the relatively high share of viewers on the main channel, because the niche channels generate only between 1.7 per cent and 4.4 per cent of audience share. Furthermore, the main channel's share has been declining since 2007, and in 2019 it was 25 per cent and adding to this problem the household penetration is declining too (*TV 2 Public Service-redegørelse 2018* 2019).

Another reason for this 'one-way street' strategy is connected to *the model* applied by TV 2/Danmark in order to segment the audience. As with DR, a kind of 'mother ship' model is applied, with mixed programming and the mainstream audience as the target group. This is very different from the model applied to the Danish market by the commercial provider Nordic Entertainment Group (NENT), for example. NENT uses 'a portfolio of equals' model, where all channels are aimed at the same commercially important target group (those aged 15–55), but with differences in content that make cross-promotion more relevant. In line with the segmentation model applied by TV 2/Danmark, the *segmentation tools* it uses are a third reason. TV 2/Danmark uses age (TV 2/Zulu for the 15- to 39-year-olds, and TV 2/Charlie for those aged over 55) as a segmentation tool, as well as channels with mono-generic content (24/7 news, lifestyle and sports). This strategy results in a kind of segmentation that leaves the main channel to fight for a commercially interesting mainstream target group who will watch a schedule of mixed programming, which makes cross-promotion less relevant. DR's segmentation tools are a mixture of age (e.g. two channels for children, and one for young adults), and a nexus between lifestyle segments and mixed programming, with relatively sharp generic profiles (documentaries and current affairs; (high) culture and art house films).

To sum up this first trend towards *divergence,* TV 2/Danmark seems to be positioned somewhere between offering viewers a choice of products within its portfolio and needing to hold on to a large and commercially important mainstream segment of the audience, because of the role of the traditional business model: selling eyeballs. As a provider that is funded by public funding, DR is inclined to behave as a *curator*, and to be indifferent to whether the viewer switches channels or drops the linear flow, as long as he or she stays within the DR portfolio. Furthermore, DR may be indifferent about which device or distribution channel is used.

Trend II: the informative value and relationship-building in continuity

The continuity texts produced by the two channels are characterised by two common and concurrent principles: first, compression of information, and second, accumulation of information. The aim is to save time and to keep viewers waiting for as short a time as possible for a (new) programme to start. For TV 2, airing advertisements and sponsorship announcements during the intervals leaves little time for other types of interstitials. This means that the interface layout at TV 2 depends heavily on stills, in combination with schedule outlines and the channel voice addresses. In comparison, DR1 is marked by an elaborate use of channel voice addresses, schedule outlines and, especially, trailers (between five and ten of them) that are piled up during a short (2–5 minute) interval. In particular, the use of trailers, schedule outlines and channel voice addresses, and the way these components are edited, are important to the differences between the two companies, and will be the focus of this section of the chapter.

Trailers[2]

A total of six different kinds of trailers are used, containing three different time frames – present, immediate future, and future – combined with two different (imagined) spatial frameworks – here and there.

1: here and now, in a few moments
2: here and in the immediate future, just after this programme
3: here and in the future (a few days from now, or later this season)
4: there and now, on a niche channel and/or non-linear platform
5: there and in the immediate future, on a niche channel and/or platform
6: there and in the future, on a niche channel and/or platform (including DR's radio channels).

DR1 uses what I would like to term a 'collage' strategy in its composition of the individual trailers, the schedule outline and the channel voice, following a set pattern lasting around one minute:

1:   here and now, in a few moments
2:   here and in the immediate future, just after this programme
3:   here and in the future
4:   there and now, on a niche channel and/or non-linear platform
1:   here and now, in a few moments.

However, in many of DR's continuity sequences placed around the so-called 'tent poles' (Eastman and Ferguson 2009) of the schedule with high audience shares, such as the Sunday drama series, the Danish version of the reality game show *The Great Bake Off* and the main newscasts, there are very high numbers of trailers accumulated. An example is this three-minute sequence from Sunday 9 November at 7:57 pm:

1:   here and now, in a few moments
2:   here and in the immediate future
3:   here and in the future
3:   here and in the future
3:   here and in the future
3:   here and in the future
5:   there and in the future
4:   there and now
4:   there and now
4:   there and now
1:   here and now.

The sequence combines 'one-way street,' 'crossroads' and 'roundabout,' and the sense of the chronology of this information (what is on next?) is almost dissolved, because the temporal and spatial deixis in the discourse (when and where) shifts at a very rapid pace. However, it may leave the impression of an abundance of content on offer, which is promoted by the channel voice. Furthermore, parts of the *content* of these trailers are repeated, with small variations, several times during prime time, adding to the impression of a dissolved chronology.

In comparison to DR1, the temporal-spatial construction of continuity at TV 2 is much simpler, partly because of the limited use of trailers. When used, only type 1, type 2 and type 3 trailers occur frequently; on rare occasions, type 4 or type 5 trailing is added for immediate and future programming on the niche channels TV 2/Fri or TV 2/Charlie, or the streaming service, TV 2 Play. The obvious reason is that time for promotion and relationship-building is scarce, because the blocks of advertisements and the many announcements of the sponsors for the programme just shown, future programmes and the upcoming programme have to be placed in the breaks between programmes. Instead of piling up trailers, TV 2 puts the weight on a chronology of shifting explicit narrator identities: the channel voice, the block of advertisements labelled by a jingle and the sponsors labelled by special voice-overs. TV 2 uses a split-screen strategy during the credits, to promote the next programme, in order to save time:

However, this kind of information compression, or invasion of the interstitial into the programmes proper (Ellis 2011), is also used elaborately by DR1. All in all, DR1 has radically intensified its use of trailers, and perhaps this has been done to such a point that the informative value – information about what is on the schedule next – is compromised.

The channel voice persona

In line with the differences found in the number and variety of trailers used, the use of the channel voice represents a profound difference between the two providers. As Stigel (2004: 30) points out, in Danish television the channel voice is the explicit yet invisible representation of the provider (Van den Bulck and Enli 2014), and the use of the institutional and inclusive pronoun, 'we,' is the typical mode of address. Presently, the first-person singular pronoun, 'I,' has been added to the pronouns used by the channel voice at both channels. An example is the verbal reaction of the channel voice, just after showing a trailer for the Sunday night historical drama, *1864*, in which one of the main characters says: 'I am sure that there will soon be a sign from God':

> Channel voice (female): I am not able to tell whether there will be a sign from God, however, the most horrible side of the war shows itself in the fifth episode of *1864*. Watch it shortly...
>
> (9.11.2014 19:58)

In addition to the use of 'I,' the many 'crossroads' and 'roundabouts' in the continuity sequences at DR1 mean that the explicitly addressed viewer is not always the same unit. The second person singular pronoun, 'you,' is frequently used, sometimes for a member of a special target group in the audience. An example is the collection of trailers and channel voice addresses to children when Friday night's long-running programme *Disney Sjov* ['Disney Fun'] is over, at 19:58. A 'crossroads' to the children's channel, DR Ultra, follows the programme, promoting an event organised by DR Ultra around the children's Christmas serial in 24 episodes, *Tidsrejsen* ['The Journey through Time'], in December (DR1 14.11. 2014). This increases the focus on the channel voice as an independent television persona talking to shifting, individual viewers and having qualities normally found only among programme hosts in genres such as talk shows and quiz shows. Furthermore, DR's staging of the channel voice as a persona is intense. First, the DR1 channel voice talks much more than TV 2's, as this example from both channels on Sunday 9 November illustrates:

DR1, 20:56: Channel voice (female) during credits for the serial *1864*:

It can be increasingly difficult to keep track of all the characters in the serial *1864*. However, we will help you [second person singular pronoun/SPSP] to do so. With just a few clicks, you [SPSP] can get an overview of all the characters and their interrelationships at dr.dk/1864. And, in a few moments: from the war against the Germans, we will move on to the celebration of the fall of the Berlin Wall. Today it is exactly 25 years since the East Germans were able to freely cross the border to the West, and in *21Søndag* [the Sunday news at 21.00], in a little while, there will be pictures of the atmosphere directly from Berlin. And here there will also be news about the case of one of the biggest recent scandals of the corporate world ... that is, the bankrupt OWBunker. Kim Bildsøe Lassen [news anchor] asks how it is possible for this to happen again and again, and whether we have learned anything from past history. Join us in watching this in a little while. Later tonight something unexpected happens in the crime series about Annika Bengtzon... [New trailer is shown, and the channel voice address is intersected by trailers that continue for another 3½ minutes.]

TV 2, 20:54: Channel voice (female) during credits for *Badehotellet* ['The beach hotel']: We will be ready with a brand, new weather report in a moment. And after that, you [SPSP] can join the journey to the moon, Pandora... [split-screen of trailer for *Avatar*, and credits and schedule outline take over].

There is much less friendly, self-promotional discourse directed at the viewers on TV 2. TV 2 is far more focussed on short announcements of upcoming and future content in the present time slot of the schedule, to make the viewers stay tuned during the advertisements, and to hand over to the other institutional voices in the schedule: the advertisers and the sponsors. Furthermore, to save time, the channel voice is skipped, and the programme hosts in the trailers address the viewers directly. As a consequence, the two channels differ with regard to the weight given to delivering the stand-alone entertaining qualities of the channel voice persona (Johnson 2013; Stigel 2004). On DR1, the channel voice persona tries to present the provider as good (para-social) company, and the first way of doing this is by witty links between the speech and the audio-visual material shown. An example of this strategy is a pun on the content in the trailer for the Swedish crime series, *Wallander*:

DR1 22:30: Channel voice (male):

> *Deadline* [a highbrow, late night news and political debate talk show] is on DR2. Here at DR1 we start off the late part of the evening with a crime show about a neighbourhood watch team taking its job a little too seriously. Wallander is on the case, and it seems straightforward [in Danish: 'in front of your right leg'].

During this speech, the trailer shows the main character, Kurt Wallander, finding a right leg in a rubbish skip, which turns out to be the right leg of a mannequin (Figure 3.4).

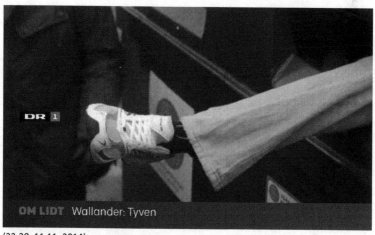

(22:30, 11.11. 2014)

Figure 3.4 Para-social company.

The DR1 channel voice also tries to build the experience of a *co-viewer relationship* with the intended viewer, by being emotionally synchronised with the content of programmes, and transmitting trailers that mirror the feelings the viewer is expected to have. An example is at 7.55 pm 12 November. A male voice on the DR1 channel addresses the intended viewer with the following words and audio-visual material: 'Yes, bon appétit!' [A ironic comment directed at the hosts and guests of the previous talk show eating cooked insects during the credits of the show]. An assumed shared feeling of disgust is emphasised as a reaction to the actions in the programme just broadcast. Another typical mode of address used to achieve this co-viewer relationship is to comment on what has been said, as in the example above, where the channel voice, as an 'I,' comments on the statement of a character in the trailer for *1864*. The shifting intonations of the channel voice are used to strengthen this position as a co-viewer. The sample from 2014 is crammed with this kind of communicative behaviour, and it leaves the impression of a humanised provider, eager to build a smooth, sociable and almost intimate emotional relationship with the individual viewer.

To sum up, with the exception of the use of 'I,' the delivery of the channel voice persona on TV 2 is very much like the persona found by Stigel (2004). This suggests that the traditional business model of linear television implemented at TV 2 may have a conservative impact, preventing the development of the channel persona for promotional purposes. On the other hand, the institutional persona is less dominant and self-promoting, and less eager to please. The informative value of what is said may even be higher, because of the simplicity of the continuity sequences produced by TV 2. In comparison, the strategy at DR1 in these ephemeral texts may be seen as a manifestation of a clash between the fundamental principles guiding public service television under the regulatory framework in Denmark. On the one hand, the obligation is to secure universal *access* to the content, and to offer *diversity* in content and in target group appeal. On the other hand, the obligation is to produce a mixed programming schedule that translates into an ideal of *mixed viewing*.

Trend III: cultivating company values in continuity

The third major trend in the communicative behaviour found in the continuity sequences is a common emphasis on *egalitarian values*. Both companies seem to be eager to place themselves at eye level with the viewers, cultivating an atmosphere of personal and sociable contact between the provider and its audience branding the channel identity (Johnson 2012). However, this is done in very different ways.

TV 2's strategy is marked by two fundamental approaches. First, the provider's contact with the TV 2 viewers is emphasised. This is shown in the many live audio-visual snippets leading into and out of the commercial breaks in the schedule. These snippets show real situations from the everyday lives of ordinary Danes, and they all contain cute emotional situations such as fun between kids and parents, family pets performing tricks or the kids playing. Every snippet is provided with information on who the people in the picture are, and where in Denmark they live. A similar version of this is used in connection with bank holidays. An example from the 2014 sample is the snippets used on 10 November, Martinmas displaying how the traditional dinner (duck) is being prepared in many different parts of Denmark on this particular evening (Figure 3.5).

Figure 3.5 TV 2 snippets.

First of all, the snippets support the existence of an actual relationship between the viewers and the provider, and not just a para-social dynamic. TV 2's otherwise conservative, generic profile embraces the digital era by giving access to the top level of the discursive hierarchy. Second, they all support a conceptualisation of the viewers as heterogeneous, with regional and local cultural identities, in line with the provincial identity of the provider: TV 2/Danmark's headquarters are situated outside the capital, and it has a network of eight regionally based news providers. At the same time, they support a conceptualisation of the viewers as sharing a homogeneous socio-cultural identity: we are all Danes celebrating this Christian holiday in the same way across the regions; this is in line with the mainstream channel identity of TV 2. Third, national and cultural cohesion is underscored by the fact that all these snippets are user-generated content from the tv2.mindag site ['tv2 my day'] at the website tv2.dk (Figure 3.6).

Until 2017 the viewers uploaded videos of their daily lives, and on the site it was possible to view the video clips uploaded by others. This strategy of including the viewer in the construction of continuity may also serve to bridge the gap between the commercial and the editorial dimension of continuity at TV 2, and to play down the commercially dominated discourse; this is especially true of the shifts between the many different sender identities at work. The value profile of the identity branding at TV 2 is continued in the *All that we share*-campaign from 2017 to the present. Snippets and four-minute videos with the

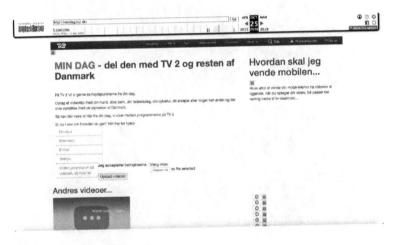

Figure 3.6 Min dag website.

common theme 'same but different' presented encounters among real-life Danes.[3]

The efforts at TV 2 to construct the impression of a *mirrored identity* between provider and viewer are not part of the communicative behaviour found in the continuity sequences at DR1. The egalitarian values there are promoted by the emphasis put on the roles of *curator* and *co-viewer*, serving the choices of the individual viewer, and sharing his or her emotional experience. In this way, the audience is conceptualised as a heterogeneous phenomenon, and the provider–user relationship is created to serve and share these differences in taste, content preferences and emotions. However, compared to TV 2's strategy, the relationship functions only as a para-social relationship, and, in addition, there is a trend towards conceptualising the viewers as a mass phenomenon. An example of this ambiguity is the portraits of the imagined viewers, presented in snippets placed randomly and very infrequently among the many trailers and channel logos. These snippets show slow-motion clips of ordinary people walking along the streets, riding bicycles and coming out of shops, for example, all in an urban environment (Figure 3.7).

The people shown are anonymous representatives of a *potential* audience, and not the viewers of DR1. The clips are provider-created promotional material, and not user-generated content. In these interstitials, the heterogeneous community of viewers addressed by DR1 remains an anonymous mass of city inhabitants from nowhere. There

Figure 3.7 DR1 snippets.

is no display of contact, either between the inhabitants, or between the provider and the inhabitants, and the provider is positioned as an observer who is unnoticed by the city inhabitants.

Conclusion: a new 'golden age'?

The three trends in the changes to 'continuity' highlight growing *differences* between the two companies who dominate the Danish television market with a combined share of 76 per cent (2018). The immediate conclusion is that the communicative behaviour characterising the on-air schedule genre at DR1 makes the channel stand out as a provider embracing the multi-channel and multi-platform possibilities of the digital era, even if the cross-promotion to the streaming service is rather modest. DR, and perhaps others from the small group of public service media (PSM) companies in the world that are 100 per cent funded by taxation or a licence fee, seems to have the upper hand in genre adaption of adapting to the viewers' extended choices and enhanced content control. The public service obligation of DR in the present Danish media policy is to make its content available and accessible on all relevant platforms in the overall media environment. By comparison, TV 2/Danmark's main channel seems to follow a more traditional strategy, and one of the core explanations for this conservatism is the impact of the limiting of the public service obligations to only the main channel, and the effect of the business model inherited from the pre-digital era. This seems to be preventing TV 2 from developing the many communicative functions of continuity in new ways, and from promoting its identity as a PSM provider instead of a traditional broadcaster. As a consequence, TV 2's ability to meet its public service obligations could become more difficult in the coming years.

DR1's enormous emphasis on promoting and branding the company's many individual channels and services on offer, and on scaling up the emotional provider–user relationship, means that continuity runs the risk of destroying itself. It turns into seemingly endless, self-serving promotion of the provider, instead of serving the basic needs of the audience for information. As pointed out, the informative dimension has become more difficult to comprehend, and continuity demands more attention by the viewers and is swamped with replays of the same trailers. This is somewhat paradoxical in a media environment marked by enhanced user control, and with an enormous amount of content and number of channels available. In this way, DR1's communicative behaviour may hurt DR's image, because it might annoy the large majority of viewers who are watching linear television, often accessed via the streaming service, and waiting for the (next) programme to start. In comparison to DR, TV 2's conservative genre profile supports an institutional ethos of stability and simplicity, as well as accessibility, community and sociability, with much less weight on the promotional needs of the provider. This may serve the image of TV 2, and silence its commercial competitors in the Danish market. However, the commercial interstitials are taking up a lot of the time, and whether this is a feasible survival strategy for attracting viewers to commercially funded public service television in the long run is questionable. In Chapter 4 these questions will be addressed from the perspective of the changing viewing habits.

Notes

1 In Chapter 4 the sample from 2016 shows a similar pattern. However, DR1 is currently (2019) putting a bit more effort in cross promoting the streaming service, and especially the content for DR3, the youth channel turning into a online only service in 2020. According to media planner Mikkel Andersen, TV 2, the use of roundabouts and the cross promotion of TV 2 Play has also become a bit more frequent in 2019 at the main channel. The reason given is that the main channel is becoming increasingly important in promoting the niche channels and the streaming service in order to keep up subscriptions to the TV 2 channel bundles and to avoid growing churn rates. This will be elaborated in Chapters 5 and 6.
2 In this chapter, I use the generic term, 'trailer' for all kinds of moving images that promote upcoming programmes.
3 The video from the *All that we share*-campaign 2019 is accessible at https://www.youtube.com/watch?v=UQ15cqP-K80

References

Bruun, H. (2018) License Fees, Platform Neutrality, and Public Service obligation. In D. Johnson (ed.) *From Networks to Netflix. A Guide to Changing Channels*. New York: Routledge, pp. 77–84.

Caldwell, J. T. (2003) Second Shift Media Aesthetics. Programming, Interactivity, and User Flows. In A. Everett and J. T. Caldwell (eds.) *New Media. Theories and Practices of Digitextuality*. New York: Routledge.

DR's public service- kontrakt for 2019–2023 (2018) København: Kulturministeriet.

Eastman, S. T. and Ferguson, D. A. (2009) *Media Programming Strategies and Practices*. Boston: Wadsworth Cengage learning.

Ellis, J. (2011) Interstitials: How the 'Bits in Between' Define the Programmes. In P. Grainge (ed.) *Ephemeral Media. Transitory Screen Culture from Television to YouTube*. London: Palgrave, pp. 59–69.

Ihlebæk, K., Syvertsen, T. and Ytreberg, E. (2014) Keeping Them and Moving Them: TV Scheduling in the Phase of Channel and Platform Proliferation. *Television & New Media*, 15(5), pp. 470–486.

Johnson, C. (2013) The Continuity of 'Continuity': Flow and the Changing Experience of Watching Broadcast Television. *Key Words*, 11, pp. 1–23.

Johnson, C. (2012) *Branding Television*. London: Routledge.

Lassen, J. M. (2018) *DRs tv-virksomhed i forandring: programflade, portefølje og platforme*. Københavns Universitet. Unpublished PhD dissertation.

Tilladelse til TV 2 Danmark A/S til at udøve public service-programvirksomhed 2019–2023. (2018) København: Kulturministeriet.

Stigel, J. (2004) TV's egenreklame og kanalstemmen. *MedieKultur*, 37, pp. 24–37.

Van den Bulck, H. and Enli, G. S. (2014). Bye, Bye "Hello Ladies?": In-vision Announcers as Continuity Technique in a European Postlinear Television Landscape: The Case of Flanders and Norway. *Television and New Media*, 15(5), pp. 453–469.

4 The implied viewer of 'continuity'

Introduction

In Chapter 3 three trends in the genre development of the on-air schedule were highlighted. In many ways the linear television paradigm dominates the communicative interface. It puts an enhanced emphasis on cross-promotion by adding the spatial dimension to scheduling and on the importance of branding the company in the market for audio-visual content. Especially television companies similar to DR with a platform neutral obligation and a business model independent of commercial income are able to explore how to 'herd' the audience within the company's portfolio of linear channels and non-linear services. By comparison commercially funded public service television like TV 2 seem to have a much more conservative approach and with an emphasis on promoting the companies' traditional brand values. All in all, the business models and the kind of cultural-political obligations the companies have to meet have an impact on the communicative strategies. Furthermore, across the two companies the conceptualisation of the audience is very much embedded in the linear television paradigm, even if the tax-funded public service television company DR is embracing new ways of 'herding' the audience.

In this chapter this fairly traditional conceptualisation of the audience will be further explored across public service and commercial television. To take on the new competition and to address changing viewer habits, many television companies have included different kinds of streaming services in their portfolios and they are also eager users of social media in the struggle to reach and attract the viewers. This development is, however, a double challenge to the dominating business model in the industry: the commercial break. As an integrated part of the on-air schedule of linear television and what the industry calls 'continuity,' this business model is presently under threat owing to the tensions between a linear and a non-linear television paradigm. However, recent explanations of the way in which different television companies navigate the tensions between these two paradigms have pointed to the *resilience* of the traditional linear television paradigm in the re-configuration of 'continuity' and of the on-air schedule produced by the television companies (Johnson 2013, 2017; Enli and Van den Bulck 2014; Ihlebæk et al. 2014; Barra and Scaglioni 2017). Like the findings presented in Chapter 3 this chapter adds to this body of work in television studies, contributing in particular to a discussion of the kind of *implied viewer* that is being produced by the broadcasters.

The chapter presents the results from a comparative analysis of the kind of 'continuity' that is produced by the four biggest television broadcasters in Denmark, with a combined share of television viewing of 95 per cent of the digitally advanced Danish media market (European Commission, DESI report 2018). As elaborated in Chapter 1 the access to high-speed broadband connections (100 Mbit/s), which are important for the use of audio-visual media of high quality, is 93 per cent (Agency of Culture and Palaces, *Mediernes udvikling I Danmark: Internetbrug og enheder* 2019: 4). Potentially, this level of access makes the Danish market a test bed for studying the tensions between the two television paradigms because it is increasingly the case that Danish viewers are no longer forced to watch time-structured television schedules – they have other options. The analysis will show how the communicative behaviour of the four main channels, in different ways, is part of what I call a traditional *delay economy* associated with linear television which relies heavily on the patience of the implied viewers. The chapter then discusses how the delay economy might be challenged by what I call an emerging *impatience culture*. The chapter suggests that the experience of gaining instant access to desired audio-visual content and the proliferation of digital games on different devices contribute in particular to a set of expectations among the viewers that is a possible challenge to the delay economy. However, the television companies are powerful industrial and cultural-political agents that try to produce their own futures by catering to and co-shaping the habits of the viewers. They are not just the victims of disruptive new competitors and technological change but active agents in shaping the future of the industry in which the linear and non-linear overlap or co-exist. In line with these claims the chapter finally suggests that the delay economy and the on-air schedule, including the interstitials of 'continuity,' as a televisual genre might hold attractions important to the viewers that will shape the future of the medium in the digital era.

As argued in Chapter 1 the third tier of the schedule as a televisual genre: the on-air schedule is very much a child of the key characteristics of the linear television paradigm. It performs a list of *communicative functions* in the provider-viewer relationship that might be very close to what television studies have regarded as the basic characteristics of television as a medium. Two of these communicative functions will be highlighted in this chapter in order to discuss the clash between an evolving set of viewer expectations towards television in the digital era supported by the industry itself and the implied viewer of 'continuity.' First, 'continuity' aims to be a televisual text that informs the viewers of upcoming content, holds the viewers' attention during these intermissions and even attracts new viewers for the upcoming content. The text produced strives to tackle the tension between the schedule and the programmes on the one hand, and the time viewers spend waiting for the next programme to begin on the other hand. Second, during these intermissions, which are probably primarily regarded as *waiting time* by the viewers, providers *promote* themselves and their products in accordance with the traditional *business model*: commercial breaks including sponsorship announcements.

Even if the schedule is still fundamental to the way a television company communicates its content to the majority of its audience and makes a revenue the viewing habits in the population are changing. There are huge differences between the European markets, and viewing of traditional linear television in Denmark is well below the European rather steady average of 3:38 hours a day (The European Broadcasting Union: *Audience Trends* 2019: 2). In 2018, Danes spent 2:22 hours a day on average watching television, dwindling from an all-time high of 3:18 hours in 2010.[1] Furthermore, the young audiences are spearheading this trend. In 2018 the average viewing time of 12–18-year-old Danes was 37 minutes and among the 19–34-year-olds the average viewing time was 1:09 hours a day (Agency for Culture and Palaces: *Mediernes udvikling i Danmark: TV og Streaming* 2019: 17). There is no data available that *includes* the use of transnational Over The Top services (OTT) and social media, and the decline in the use of audio-visual content might well be less if these companies were participating. However, data on the use of streaming (OTTs, YouTube, broadcasters' steaming services) shows a weekly reach of 57 per cent in the population (+12) in 2018, and 88 per cent of the 19–34-year-olds (Agency for Culture and Palaces: *Mediernes udvikling i Danmark: TV* 2019: 38). The increase in streaming activity is present in all age groups. Furthermore, to recap from Chapter 1 OTTs like Netflix have a very strong position on the Subscription-Video-On-Demand (SVOD) market in Denmark.

Netflix was introduced in 2012 and 39 per cent of the Dane use the service every week. Compared to the use of the streaming services of the broadcasters in 2018, 33 per cent of the population (+12) use DR's streaming service DRTV included in the tax-funded public service media in Denmark every week. Nordic Entertainment Group's (NENT) ViaPlay is second with a reach of 16 per cent and TV 2's streaming service TV 2 Play is third with 15 per cent (Agency for Culture and Palaces: *Mediernes udvikling i Danmark: Streaming* 2018: 18).

The changing patterns in television viewing in the digitally advanced Danish market (particularly among young audiences) are, as mentioned, a challenge to the traditional business model in the television industry. From the perspective of the broadcasters, 'continuity' was and still is about how television broadcasters struggle to make the audience stay tuned as long as possible by using strategic and tactical textual efforts (Eastman and Ferguson 2013). The on-air schedule and 'continuity' in traditional linear television schedules need to create *delay* in such a way that the commercial and/or editorial breaks between the programmes result not in a loss of viewers but ideally built expectations and attract more viewers instead. As a consequence, and seen from the viewer's point of view, 'continuity' is packed with many different ways to make the viewer *wait* for access to attractive *new* content: e.g. the fixed time structures of the schedule (prime time, day, week, month, etc.); the way content is serialised and narrated in instalments; the systematic use of reruns in order to fill 24/7 schedules and maximise audience ratings; the holding back of new content due to appear any time within the next few months. In short, 'continuity' in traditional linear television draws on the *patience* of the implied viewers, and the temporal structuring of the channel is governed by what I term a *delay economy*. The characteristics of the kind of 'continuity' produced by the four television companies navigating between the two television paradigms at work within their portfolios will be highlighted in the following section of the chapter.

Continuity – and a little change

As mentioned in the introduction to this chapter, several contributions have already underlined the resilience of the linear television paradigm in the television industry, and 'flow' is a potent concept which is still very much in use in the industry. Constructing a channel 'flow' that retains the viewers who are already watching, as well as attracting new viewers, is still the fundamental communicative function of the on-air schedule and of 'continuity' in a competitive cross-platform media landscape. As findings from Chapter 3 suggest, the driving force is the business model of linear television: commercial breaks. The result is that DR stands out as far more non-linear and much more oriented to the idea of the user's choice. This communicative strategy is supported by the public service obligation to provide access to content regardless of the platform used. In this way, commercial funding has a conservative effect on the construction of 'continuity' regardless of the technology that the companies use. This trend is also supported by Johnson's analysis (2017) of how the interface of the ITV Hub is structured in interplay with the linear channels, and in particular by the logics of broadcasting. These findings from research into contemporary developments in the television industry question any simple distinctions between the linear and the non-linear television paradigm, making a clear-cut move towards a non-linear television paradigm seem less probable. Instead, the findings indicate that broadcasters are navigating the tensions in order to secure profitable and/or cultural-political important user flows.

In the following section of the chapter I will add to the results of this body of research by presenting the findings from the comparative analysis of how 'continuity' in the on-air schedules of the four biggest television companies on the Danish market is employed to address the viewer. The sample used is the 'continuity' broadcast by the main channels of these companies (DR1, TV 2, TV3 and Kanal 5) from 7 pm to midnight during the period 8–14 February 2016. The design of the methodological approach is mirroring the one used in the study of the two public service companies presented in Chapter 3. The sample can come across as a bit old; however, the arguments for the cogency of the findings are as described and elaborated in Chapter 3. The analysis focusses on how *delay* is presupposed in very different ways among the four companies. The chapter will then discuss the question of the conceptualisation of the audience behind these communicative strategies and their viability in view of the radical changes in the way television content is accessed on the Danish market. A part from the two public service television companies on the Danish market the two important commercial companies are: NENT, and Discovery Networks Denmark distributed by satellite or by cable and the DTT network. Currently, all four companies have large portfolios of five to thirteen television channels each (2019). They also offer one or more streaming services each to provide on-demand and live access to the content they produce. All these companies have extensive websites, and they are all eager users of social network media. This focus on producing cross-media television content is driven by the fact that Danes are frequent users of social media – especially Facebook, which supports 3.9 million Danish profiles, and YouTube used by 50 per cent of the population every week. There are, however, important differences between the four major television companies. As described in Chapter 3 DR is an independent, publicly owned institution, while TV 2/Danmark is a publicly owned limited company. NENT and Discovery are the Danish branches of multinational corporations operating in many other countries, too. Both broadcast to Denmark from the United Kingdom in order to avoid Danish television advertising laws, which are stricter than those formulated by British (or European Union) regulations. TV 2/Danmark, NENT and Discovery are all funded by advertising and subscriptions. But under Danish law, TV 2/Danmark is only allowed to place commercials *between* programmes. This limitation stems from the public service obligation of TV 2/Danmark's main channel and eight regional news affiliates, and advertising made up 46 per cent of the company's revenue in 2018. TV 2/Danmark and DR have a combined share of viewing of 76 per cent (DR 37 and TV 2/Danmark 39 per cent). The two commercial companies have a share of viewing of 10 per cent each (2018).

The delay economy of 'the big four'

Given these important differences between the four television companies in terms of ownership, cultural-political frameworks and obligations, and in terms of business models and market position, the forms of 'continuity' produced for the four main channels display both similarities and differences in regards to *how* the implied audience is asked to wait for content, and in terms of *what* they are asked to wait for.

Waiting time

Across the four main channels, the intermissions between the programmes or parts of the programmes make the implied viewers wait for the next programme to start or to continue. Table 4.1 shows the differences between the four during the period 8–14 February 2016 and between 7 pm and midnight:

The time spent on intermissions includes commercial breaks and sponsorship announcements for all the channels apart from DR1. TV3 and Kanal 5 make their implied viewer wait for a programme to continue many times during each broadcast, but each break is shorter than the breaks employed by TV 2 because TV3 and Kanal 5 are allowed to interrupt their programmes. The high frequency of these intermissions means that the shortest sections of programmes are not much longer than the longest intermissions. Here is an example of this situation: one hour of prime time on TV3 during which the programme

Table 4.1 Waiting time

Main channel public service (PS) – commercial (COM)	DR1 PS	TV2 PS/COM	TV3 COM	Kanal 5 COM
Number of intermissions 7–12 pm, 8–14 February 2016	37	61	231	242
Total broadcast time for intermissions in minutes	82	370	579	582
Per cent of broadcast time	3	15	23	23
Average broadcast time of intermissions in minutes	2.2	6.1	2.5	2.4
Length of intermissions in minutes	1–4	1–9	1–7	1–8

was interrupted by three intermissions lasting three to seven minutes (Figure 4.1).

Sixteen minutes of this hour in prime time was spent on non-programmes, and the commercial channels expected the viewers to stay tuned during these often rather long and frequent intermissions. This is what commercial television has been like for decades, and the digital era has not brought any changes. Furthermore, and as illustrated in Table 4.1, not only TV3 but all the main channels do not seem to have any problem in making the viewers wait for a long time before

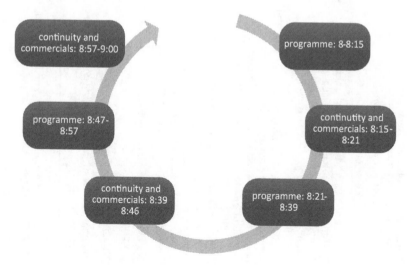

Figure 4.1 Broadcast hour TV3, 8–9 pm.

Table 4.2 Promotional interstitials

Promotional interstitial, 7–12 pm, 8–14 February 2016	DR1 PS	TV2 PS/COM	TV3 COM	Kanal 5 COM
Number of *'Crossroads' to one **immediate** content alternative on a linear channel	9	5	4	4
Number of *'Roundabouts' to two or more **immediate** content alternatives on linear channels	13	0	0	0
Number of interstitials promoting **future** content on the **main linear channel**	129	223	238	336
Number of interstitials promoting **Future** content on **other** linear channels in the portfolio	54	18	41	87
Number of interstitials promoting the streaming services (label on-screen and/or channel voice directing the viewer towards the streaming service's content)	1 (part of the tax: DRTV)	15 (**SVOD: TV 2Play)	121 (**AVOD: ViaFree) 9 (SVOD: TV3 Play/Via Play)	126 (AVOD/SVOD: DPlay)
Number of interstitials promoting the website	1	6	0	0
Number of interstitials promoting an app	8	6	0	0
Number of interstitials promoting content on social media (label on screen)	0	1 (Facebook)	0	61 (Twitter # for the same programme)

*'Crossroad': interstitials promoting one immediate alternative programme on another linear channel in the company's portfolio. 'Roundabouts': interstitials promoting two or more immediate alternative programmes.
**SVOD: subscription video on demand; AVOD: advertisement-funded video on demand.

continuing the programmes. The differences between the commercially funded channels, the channel with tax funding and the two channels with public service obligations are, however, huge. Tax-funded DR1 is the channel with the fewest and shortest intermissions, even though they still make the viewers wait for a relatively long time between the programmes. DR uses the intermissions for the cross-promotion of programmes and channels. TV 2 is second to DR in terms of the number and length of the intermissions. As mentioned above, this is because TV 2 is only allowed under Danish law to have breaks between programmes – not breaks during programmes.

The temporalities of promotional interstitials

Across the commercially funded channels, intermissions are used mainly to broadcast commercials and sponsorship announcements. This means that there are huge differences between the ways in which the four channels use self-promotional communication during intermissions. Table 4.2 shows the differences.

The tax-funded public service television channel DR1 uses self-promotional tools that set this channel very much apart from the other three. All the intermissions feature trailers and on-screen schedules for programmes on different channels in DR's portfolio as alternatives to what will be shown on DR1 'now.' In Chapter 3 I call this self-promotional technique a 'crossroads' or 'roundabout,' encouraging the viewer to continue viewing on another linear channel. A 'roundabout' includes trailers for up to four immediate alternatives to the programme that will be shown on DR1 'now.' These interstitials add a spatial dimension to the channel flow, making the implied viewers for the upcoming programme on the channel wait – and is also a kind of service for viewers who want to zap.

TV 2 and the two commercial channels have a very limited use of crossroads and do not use roundabouts. Instead, they prefer to point the implied viewer in the direction of their *streaming service* to catch up on episodes from the series they have just watched on the linear channel. In my sample, TV 2 offers access to a *new* episode of a series that has just been shown, a preview to reduce the waiting time. In the sample, this happens 20 times and promotes the next episode of three different series: one fiction, one reality game show and one documentary. Kanal 5 uses this tool only once during the week. Apart from this tool, the streaming services only make content available that has already been shown (or is going to be shown) on linear television at the same time. If the viewer pays for the SVOD services on offer, the huge number of intermissions on the linear channels can be avoided and viewers are also given the chance to access content via other devices, e.g. via Apple TV. TV3 also offers a free streaming service, ViaFree, but the commercial breaks are then included and there is only a limited range of genres, and no new content is available. DR's streaming service DRTV is also funded by taxation; but even though there are no financial or legal problems in doing so, DR1 seldom cross-promote their streaming service in the 'continuity' sequences. DR1 does not promote previews either, even though this is a tool used on the streaming service. This behaviour might be due to an attempt to avoid political discussions in Denmark during the Winter of 2016 about the balance between the private and the public media sector.

As shown in Table 4.2, all four channels have a very large amount of promotion of *future content* on their main linear channels, which will also be available as live streaming on their Video on Demand (VOD) and SVOD services. However, once again there are huge differences in the ways in which this promotional activity is carried out: DR1 is the only channel that fills the waiting time by promoting programmes that will be shown *more* than one week into the future. DR1 and Kanal 5 cross-promote to other channels, whereas TV 2 and TV3 are less eager to use intermissions for this kind of cross-promotional activity. These differences between the four companies might be caused by the specific kind of portfolio they offer and the target group in question. The whole of DR1's portfolio is funded by taxation, so in one sense it does not matter which DR channel the viewers watch, whereas Kanal 5 is the mainstream and more family-oriented channel in a portfolio characterised in other respects by gender segmentation. This means that Kanal 5 may choose to cross-promote Kanal 4, which has 15–40-year-old women as its target group. TV3 is the main channel, but the sister channels are very much alike and target the same 21–50-year-old audience. For NENT using 'crossroads' would in fact be an option, but it is not used and perhaps because of this similarity among the channels. Finally, at TV 2 the important thing is to use promotion time to secure a large viewership in terms of the ratings, shares and reach of the main channel, which is the cash cow and has public service obligations to meet. High ratings are therefore also politically important, while reach is becoming increasingly important owing to the decline in linear television viewing. All three commercially funded channels try to strike a balance between commercial needs and promotional needs during their intermissions. In fact, very little time is spent on promotional interstitials on the three commercial channels. As mentioned above, the time is already almost completely taken up with commercials and sponsorship announcements, and the fear of losing the audience if the intermissions grow any longer seems to limit the use of cross-promotion. Furthermore, none of the companies can compete with companies like Netflix in terms of new content for their streaming services, so they probably need to keep their viewers using the linear channels.

Let me now summarise the points made above about the time structures of promotional interstitials across the four channels. The implied viewer is asked to wait even though the programmes have been produced and are – in principle – available. In addition to this deliberate delay, the self-promotional material for the same programmes is repeated. Examples of this general trend are the promotion of *Champions League* on TV3+, which is promoted by 15 trailers, and a new entertainment show coming soon on Kanal 5: *Lille Fredag* [Little Friday], which is promoted by 60 schedule outlines. Even though the actual time spent is relatively short, the phenomenological experience of this might be very different. The initial informative function (the building of expectations) as well as the possible entertainment value of the promotional material might fade rapidly owing to number of times these promotions are repeated. In short, the delay economy is still in operation, dominating the way in which 'continuity' is used for promotional purposes.

The temporalities of commercial interstitials

On the three commercially funded channels, the intermissions mainly consist of a block of commercials and a number of sponsorship announcements surrounding the programmes or programme instalments. TV3 and Kanal 5 are the channels with the highest number of commercial breaks and announcements of sponsorships. Table 4.3 shows the differences between the three channels from 7 pm to midnight 8–14 February 2016.

Table 4.3 Number of commercial breaks and sponsorship announcements

Number of commercial breaks and sponsorship announcements, 7–12 pm, 8–14 February 2016	*TV 2* *PS/COM*	*TV3* *COM*	*Kanal 5* *COM*
Commercial breaks	54	69	69
Sponsorship announcements	69	555	501

This means that TV3 and Kanal 5 also have the highest number of *repetitions* of commercials as well as sponsorship announcements. The possible entertainment value of the commercials will probably fade as they are repeated more frequently. The sponsorship announcements consist of small clips from known television commercials or audio-visual presentations of the sponsor's products, and they are accompanied by a voice-over announcing the name of the company and the programme it sponsors. These announcements have probably no entertainment value at all, not even the first time they are heard. Kanal 5 has up to seven of these announcements during the intermissions. In addition, the commercial interstitials face the fundamental problem that all commercials (regardless of medium) have in common: they are often an unwanted kind of information seen from the point of view of the audience. In television, commercials risk annoying the viewers and trying their patience, as documented by Ofcom's longitudinal study of adults' media lives (Ofcom, 2016: 36; Ofcom, 2017: 43). This is especially the case on TV3 and Kanal 5. As mentioned above, TV 2 is not allowed to interrupt its programmes and does not transmit the same number of intermissions during which sponsorship announcements can be repeated. Finally, TV 2 does not seem to need many repetitions of commercials and sponsorship announcements, a fact which is related to TV 2's very strong market position.

The delay economy meets an emerging impatience culture

The temporal configurations of 'continuity' show that the traditional delay economy of the linear television paradigm dominates on the four channels, particularly on the three commercially funded channels. The business model used, rather than the technology employed, seems to have a conservative effect on how these three companies construct their interactions with the audience between programmes. This means that the differences between commercial and non-commercial television are obvious. Perhaps unsurprisingly, the 100 per cent tax-funded public service channel DR1 takes the lead in guiding the implied viewer to break away from the flow of content on the main channel. However, even though this is the case, the implied viewer waiting for the content to continue on DR1 is asked to wait for a relatively long time because priority is given to self-promotional interstitials. Furthermore, the promotion of streaming services by DR as well as TV 2 is limited, and has not intensified compared to the analysis of the 2014 sample in Chapter 3. The next section of the chapter discusses whether or not sticking to the delay economy is a viable strategy for the television industry. Viewing habits are changing; and if the industry wishes to retain a viewership in future, it may have to abandon all these delays. First, the audience that the television companies are trying to attract and hold on to by using the tools of the traditional delay economy have gained enhanced control over what they watch, and when and where they watch it. This probably means that many viewers are rapidly getting used to *not* waiting for the content they want, or just waiting for a few seconds: for instance until advertisements can be skipped on a YouTube video or the countdown to the next episode of a Netflix serial is over. Increasingly, they might also expect to gain access to available content for as long as they like without unwanted interruptions or repetitions of unwanted information. As suggested by Jason Mittell after watching his own children using TiVo, future viewers will probably also expect to be able to control the flow, to speed up or stop consumption, and to move on to other kinds of content somewhere else with a single click, if they so desire (Mittell 2011). The algorithm-based personalisation used by OTTs, but to a very limited extent by commercial as well as public service television companies, might add to this development (Moe and Van den Bulck 2017: 12). It supports the *feeling* of getting an instant as well as a personally relevant offer from the television companies – just like social media providing audio-visual content and the web in general do. These different kinds of experiences of time control and instant access might undermine or just clash with the delay economy's implied viewer. The value chain policies of Netflix may accelerate this trend, given that the company does not support the traditional hold-back agreements in the television industry because the company does not have a portfolio of 24/7 schedules to fill and does not sell advertiser space either. And finally, OTTs in general do not need the temporal standardisations of content in order to fit their schedules and commercial breaks.

All in all, the audience expectations that might gradually be shaped by the elaborated use of on-demand streaming and social media do not match the implied viewer of the delay economy. A second set of cultural experiences should also be taken into consideration because it might challenge the delay economy: the proliferation of digital games on a variety of devices. We know very little about how this kind of entertainment might influence the experience of watching linear and non-linear television. However, as Evans (2015) has pointed out in her analysis of games designed for mobile phones and tablets, the gaming industry tries to monetise the impatience of the players in a different way than traditional television. The player decides when to play the game, not the producers of the game, but in many app-based freemium games the player is given the opportunity to gain access and cut waiting periods by paying. This simulates a 'get-it-now' attitude, as Evans terms it (ibid.: 578).

Nevertheless, compared to linear television, it is possible for each player to control the temporal flow because the play structure is asynchronous, which allows their attention to be intermittent (ibid.: 576). Moreover, the games are designed to fit into the schedule of the day and perhaps fill brief moments of time at the player's pleasure. As Vordere et al. (2006) argue, this kind of everyday digital entertainment gives the user the ability to engage in an activity that gives the impression of being available on request and at the player's convenience – without waiting for others to make content available. As further argued by Vordere et al., the feeling of autonomy is combined with the fact that the gameplay of these products can produce an instant feeling of personal competence because the level of difficulty in the game is always a product of the abilities of the user (ibid.: 7–8). The *feeling* of being in charge of your own time and producing your own (customised) media entertainment is probably an experience with which most contemporary television viewers are familiar and an important clue about the kind of entertaining qualities viewers of television might expect.

Conclusion: on the edge of extinction?

As suggested above, the changing horizon of expectations among the television viewers could easily produce a growing impatience with regard to the delay economy of the on-air schedule. The commercial television channels are challenged in particular, given the fact that they are extremely dependent on the business model represented by 'continuity' and therefore on the attention of young audience segments. These segments are leading the tendency to cut back on watching linear television. Furthermore, the relatively weak position of the two commercial companies on the Danish television market adds to their problems. DR, on the other hand, has the technological, cultural-political and financial muscle to recalibrate the relationship between the two television paradigms and reconceptualise the notion of the viewer in a more radical fashion. Even though there is profound insecurity about the future of the linear television paradigm in the industry, the broadcasters are powerful agents of transformation themselves, producing their own futures by co-shaping the habits of their viewers. As the analysis in this chapter shows, the professional schedulers and producers try to appropriate the non-linear paradigm and integrate it into their strategies and tactics in a way that fits the multi-platform 'ecosystems' or 'digital estates' of the television companies (Evans et al. 2017: 1; Johnson 2019). The resilience of the linear television paradigm in the genre is evident in the communicative strategies of the four companies, and this might not just be a strategy to protect the status quo. It may be a way to disrupt the distinction drawn in the industry between broadcasting and on-line, and between linear and non-linear television. In their analysis of the managerial discourse of the BBC iPlayer mentioned above, Grainge and Johnson show how the conceptualisation of its role in the organisation has changed from a catch-up service to the 'front door' to an 'entertainment destination' (2018: 35). According to the managerial discourse, the linear and the non-linear overlap.

Finally, we might also wonder why Danish audiences do not use the streaming services provided by broadcasters to a much higher degree, given the proliferation of broadband internet access in Danish households. In 2018 only 9 minutes out of 2.22 hours of daily viewing were spent on time shifted viewing (author's analysis in Kantar Gallup's database). Furthermore, the use of linear television had a weekly reach in the population (+12) of 77 per cent in 2018 (Agency of Culture and Palaces: *Mediernes udvikling i Danmark: TV og Streaming* 2019: 4). The stronghold of linear use is supported by the result of an EBU-survey of 12 European markets: 92 per cent of all viewing in 2018 was in fact done on linear television (EBU 2019: 2). In other words, why do audiences in Europe and in Denmark – myself included – still choose to use linear television? This might be a matter of time and also a generational issue, but other reasons need to be considered, too. One of these reasons might be that the streaming services are still very expensive compared to traditional cable or DTT distribution. A second is probably the dominant position of public service television on the Danish market, providing the audience with a lot of linear television containing relatively few intermissions. The difference compared with a streaming service like DRTV or TV 2 Play is therefore comparatively small. A third reason might be that the delay economy and some of the communicative functions of 'continuity' in general are in fact valued by the audience? As argued in Chapter 1 the third tier of the schedule and 'continuity' represent the communicative interface between the broadcaster and the viewer, and here we find the quintessence of the *immediacy and 'live-ness' of the television experience* as a time-structured mass medium. As pointed out by Stigel (2001) a perpetual 'here and now' is presented in which the different parts of the day (daytime, prime time, late fringe) and the week are mirrored, and to which the different temporal and spatial settings of the individual programmes (e.g. the 'here-and-now' of the talk show; the 'there-and-now 'of the television transmission of an event; the 'there-and-then' of the television drama) return. Furthermore, in the communicative interface built by 'continuity,' *the viewers' presence* is persistently recognised, e.g. by the channel voice. 'Continuity' is probably an important component of the 'anyone as someone' structure of the television experience, interlinking the private sphere of the viewer(s) and the public sphere of television in everyday life (Scannell, 1996: 14). In this way, continuity is probably a fundamental component of the 'taken-for-granted-ness' and 'dailiness' of television, as Scannell argues (1996: 9, 144). All in all, 'continuity' might still be an important aspect of the attraction of watching television, so it may survive as a televisual phenomenon.

All of this call for continued research not only into how 'continuity' as a televisual phenomenon and its production is changing in the digital era but also into its possible importance to the audience. This endeavour may help to flesh out in whose interest producing a fairly traditional on-air schedule in which the linear and non-linear co-exist and are intertwined might be. Is it a possible future trajectory for the television industry in order to maintain its economic interests? Is it a fruitful way to ensure the cultural-political importance of the medium in society in the digital era? Is it yet another testimony to the adaptability and agility of the industry that has been seen before in television history? Or will streaming kill the television industry from outside and from within because the industry is not able to survive the effects of the disruption in the long run? In order to address these questions, the following two chapters of this book will investigate the production of the schedule with a special focus on the public service company TV 2.

Note

1 The method behind these figures changed from January 2017. The present data includes live/linear as well as time-shifted use of television content from all devices, not just from a connected television set up until seven days after the initial broadcast. The streaming of content from the broadcasters' different streaming services before broadcasting (e.g. previews), on-line only content and streaming of content after that period are not included in the consolidated ratings. This change in method also makes a comparison with previous years and periods very complicated.

References

Agency of Culture and Palaces (2019) *Mediernes udvikling i Danmark: TV og Streaming*. København: Slots- og Kulturstyrelsen.

Agency of Culture and Palaces (2019) *Mediernes udvikling i Danmark: Internetbrug og enheder*. København: Slots- og Kulturstyrelsen.

Agency of Culture and Palaces (2018) *Mediernes udvikling i Danmark: Streaming*. København: Slots- og Kulturstyrelsen.

Barra, L. & Scaglioni, M. (2017) Paratexts, Italian Style: The Promotional Cultures of Italian Commercial and Pay Television Broadcasters. *Critical Studies in Television*, 12(2), pp. 156–173.

Eastman, S. T. and Ferguson, D. A. (2013) *Media Programming Strategies and Practices.* Boston: Wadsworth Cengage learning.

Enli, G. & Van den Bulck, H. (2014). Bye, Bye "Hello Ladies?": In-vision Announcers as Continuity Technique in a European Post Linear Television Landscape: The Case of Flanders and Norway. *Television and New Media,* 15(5), pp. 453–469.

European Broadcasting Union (2019) *Audience Trends. Television 2018. Public version.* Geneva: EBU.

European Commission (2019) *DESI/Digital Economy and Society Index 2018.* Brussels: EU.

Evans, E. (2015) The Economics of Free: Freemium Games, Branding and Impatience Economy. *Convergence,* 22(6), pp. 563–580.

Evans, E., Coughlan, T. and Coughlan, V. (2017) Building Digital Estates: Multiscreening, Technology Management and Ephemeral Television. *Critical Studies in Television,* 12(2), pp. 191–205.

Grainge, P. and Johnson, C. (2018). From Catch-up TV to Online TV: Digital Broadcasting and the Case of BBC iPlayer. *Screen,* 59(1), pp. 21–40. doi:10.1093/screen/hjy002.

Ihlebæk, K., Syvertsen, T. and Ytreberg, E. (2014) Keeping Them and Moving Them: TV Scheduling in the Phase of Channel and Platform Proliferation. *Television & New Media,* 15(5), pp. 470–486.

Johnson, C. (2019) *Online TV.* London: Routledge.

Johnson, C. (2017) Beyond Catch-up: VoD Interfaces, ITV Hub and the Repositioning of Television Online. *Critical Studies in Television,* 12(2), pp. 121–138.

Johnson, C. (2013) The Continuity of 'Continuity': Flow and the Changing Experience of Watching Broadcast Television. *Key Words,* 11, pp. 1–23.

Mittell, J. (2011) TiVoing Childhood: Time Shifting a Generations Concept of Television. In M. Krackman, M. Binfield, M. T. Payne, A. Perlman and B. Sebok (eds.) *Flow TV. Television in the Age If Media Convergence.* New York: Routledge, pp. 146–154.

Moe, H. and Van den Bulck, H. (2017). Public Service Media, Universality and Personalisation: Mapping Strategies and Exploring Dilemmas. *Media, Culture and Society,* 40(6), pp. 875–892.

Ofcom (2017) *Adults' Media Lives 2016: A Qualitative Study.* Wave 12 Summery Report.

Ofcom (2016) *Media Lives 2015: A Qualitative Study.* Wave 11 Summery Report.

Scannell, P. (1996) *Radio, Television and Modern Life.* London: Blackwell Publishers.

Stigel, J. (2001) Aesthetics of the Moment in Television. In G. Agger and J. F. Jensen (eds.) *The Aesthetics of Television.* Aalborg: Aalborg University Press, pp. 25–52.

Vordere, P., Steen, F. F. and Chan, E. (2006) Motivation. In J. Bryant and P. Vordere (eds.) *Psychology of Entertainment.* London: Lawrence Erlbaum Associates Publishers, pp. 3–18.

5   The changing production culture

Introduction

> The funny thing, comparing the present to the 'old days' [2004],
> is in fact that all the production processes and promotional pro-
> cesses involved have become *far* more complicated [...] In fact
> on-air television scheduling was a rather simple matter back then
> (laughs).
>
> (Head of Scheduling TV 2, Mette Rysø Johansen,
> 7.3.2016, personal interview)[1]

This is a quote from one of the many interviews conducted in the study
of the changes in the production of the on-air schedule in Danish public
service television. It expresses a general notion held by the producers:
the practices of on-air scheduling are changing and getting much more
complicated in the digital era. The traditional linear television environment that constituted the basis for this kind of production in television is gone, and a linear as well as non-linear television environment
has taken over. Among the schedulers and continuity producers there
is a sense of insecurity regarding what the future might bring, but also
a very strong will to understand and to adapt to changes, and to the
new terms of competition for the attention of the audience on the media market for audio-visual content. The aim of this chapter is to shed
some light on these changes in the *production culture* (Caldwell 2008)
of the producers: how do these professionals interpret the tensions between a well-known linear television environment and the non-linear
services included in the portfolio of the provider, and do they have an
impact on the practices and value systems guiding this kind of genre
production? The chapter presents main findings from the study at the
Danish commercially funded public service television company TV 2.
The tensions between traditional linear television and the non-linear

television services have a strong influence on the production culture among the producers, and three lessons have been learned so far. First, these tensions have an impact on the ways the work of the producers aim to support and secure the position of the *main channel* in TV 2's portfolio of channels and online services in order to hold on to and guide the viewers towards profitable user flows. As a consequence, the workflow of promoting content and the demands on the qualities of the promotional material have changed. Second, an understanding of the interplay between linear and Subscription-Video-On-Demand (SVOD) scheduling is emerging. And third, a renewed focus is put on branding the viewer-provider relationship. Based on these findings the chapter finally suggests that the contours of a new television paradigm are being produced. This paradigm is marked by the interplay between the traditional and still very influential aspects of the linear television paradigm, and an emerging non-linear television paradigm that is integrated into the work practices.

Scheduling is back in style

On-air scheduling has become an increasingly difficult task from the perspective of the multi-platform television company, and it is safe to say that the communicative functions of the on-air schedule needs to allow for the enhanced choice and content control of contemporary audiences (Van Den Bulck and Enli 2014a, 2014b). This means that the on-air schedule has to be constructed in new ways. In order to understand how this plays out in the production culture, the professional producers are regarded as powerful *genre interpreters* working in specific media systemic contexts, and in specific cultural and historic contexts. This approach is in line with my theoretical understanding of professional media production presented in Chapter 2. At TV 2 the work of the schedulers has played a profound role in securing the company's rapid and continued popularity among the Danes. The powerful position of the schedulers was (and still is) heavily supported by the organisational structure: TV 2 is a so-called desktop organisation like Channel 4 in the United Kingdom, which only produces news and sports in-house. The rest of the content is either commissioned in the television production industry in Denmark, or acquired programmes. TV 2/Danmark has a share of viewing of 39 per cent across its six channels and 25 per cent for its main channel, called TV 2, which makes TV 2/Danmark the largest provider of content on the small Danish market of 5.6 million inhabitants (*TV 2 public service redegørelse 2018* 2019: 21). As described in Chapter 3 a mixture of subscriptions and advertising revenue funds TV 2/Danmark. Danish law allows commercial breaks only *between* what are considered programmes, or in 'natural breaks' within programmes, for example at half time in a football match. This legislation applies to linear as well as on-demand audio-visual content. Furthermore, TV 2/Danmark is a limited company, entirely owned by the Danish state. It has two divisions, and they have to be kept separate financially. The first is a *public service division* that includes the main channel TV 2, which has scheduled 'windows' for the eight regional news providers that are supported by public funding. The public service obligations involve offering a mixed schedule of genres and subjects translated into the ideal of a versatile viewer, as well as a comprehensive national and the regional news service. More than 50 per cent of the content commissioned must be European, with an emphasis on the Danish language and Danish culture; and since 2014 around 70 per cent of the main channel's content was in Danish. Second, TV 2/Danmark has a large purely commercial division, TV 2 Networks, which *has no public service obligations*. This division includes the tv2.dk website, five niche channels and the TV 2 Play streaming service. The five niche channels have a share of viewing between 1.7 and 4 per cent.

All in all, TV 2/Danmark is very dependent on its main channel in order to maintain the company's political importance as a public service television provider. Furthermore, the main channel is crucial to the financial survival of the company, and this survival is dependent on the viability of the inherited business model of the linear television paradigm. TV 2 is increasingly dependent on the revenues from the cable and digital terrestrial television (DTT) distribution of the channel portfolio and on subscriptions because of the declining income from television advertisements (*TV 2 Årsrapport 2018* 2019: 7). The household penetration of TV 2's channels is, however, in decline (ibid.: 13), and the cable companies selling linear television in big bundles have also been met with new political regulations in support of extended consumer choice, e.g. a la carte-model of channels. It is predicted that the number of 'cable shavers' and perhaps even 'cable cutters' will grow in the coming years, even if only 15 per cent of the Danish population are currently 'cable cutters' (2019). This has put a stop to TV 2's strategy during the early 2000s of launching new niche channels in order to offer more advertising time and get more subscriptions from a hugely segmented small Danish audience.

The three lessons learned, briefly outlined in the introduction, will be elaborated in the following section of the chapter. They all suggest that the professional practices and values guiding the production culture are being adapted in order to secure the position of the main linear channel. This analysis is based on 18 face-to-face 1–2 hours interviews with the producers; and in situ observations of the final stage of production done by the flow-planners and the on-air execution of the live production in prime time by the continuity producers. The collection of data took place from November 2015 to June 2016, and in April 2019 mainly at the TV 2 headquarters in Odense on the island of Funen in Denmark. The following section of the chapter will start with a short introduction to on-air scheduling at TV 2 in order to provide a context for the three lessons learned.

On-air scheduling and the 'ecosystem'

The production of the on-air schedule for the main channel takes place in specialised divisions of the company: the scheduling division for the main channel works in close daily cooperation with the on-air promotion division, which is part of the marketing division at TV 2. The marketing division works like an in-house PR agency for the different channels and online services in the TV 2 portfolio, called the 'ecosystem' by the producers (former head of Media and Development, Maria Gry Henriksen, 31.5.2016, personal interview). The cooperation between the scheduling division for the main channel and the scheduling division for the streaming service is intense, as is cooperation with the head of TV 2's main channel and the head of TV 2 News. The production of the interstitials for the on-air-schedule mainly takes place in-house at TV 2, and to a limited degree in special task companies and in the production companies producing commissioned programmes for TV 2. As described in Chapter 1 the production process behind the on-air schedule that hits the screen can be broken down into the same stages that structure a live television production genre like the news, but with a very different time frame. The daily broadcast of the on-air schedule is the result of a preproduction process extending up to three years into the future. This preproduction process involves constant adjustments and re-editing of the planned production, which is optimised until it is broadcast. At TV 2 this process involves a number of computer systems in which adjustments are implemented. The main content management system is called *What's On*. The final product is called a 'playlist' for the daily broadcast. The playlist contains all the programmes and interstitials produced in a time schedule and must be followed by the live broadcast producer during transmission. This phase of the preproduction process involves monitoring audience ratings, user data and competitors closely as well as events in the outside world. An unexpected event can be a total game changer, and the playlist orchestrating the on-air schedule has to be profoundly re-edited, with all the promotional work already done being, at worst, wasted. An example of this happened during my stay at TV 2 in the early spring of 2016, when a political crisis almost caused a call for a general election. This was going on during the broadcasting of a high-priority promotional campaign in the on-air schedule, and on other platforms, for a broadcast of a prime-time documentary serial that exposed the influence the imams have in the Muslim community in Denmark. If the crisis had resulted in a call for a general election, the promotional campaign would have been wasted, and for political reasons the serial had to be rescheduled.

First lesson: new promotional workflows and increased quality demands

The preproduction process outlined above and the work done are described as 'the engine room of television' (Head of logistics Jørgen Badstue, 8.6.2016, personal interview): without it the ship is not able to sail, so to speak. The core challenge in the production culture is to produce an audience of scale and commercial value for the linear main channel by learning how to harness the promotional advantages in the TV 2 ecosystem. In 2016 the head of scheduling at the streaming service TV 2 Play, Kurt Holm Jensen, describes the relationship as follows: 'The way it looks at the moment (2016), TV 2 Play is what you might call a shadow service for TV 2's main channel. But Play also supports TV 2 Zulu because the young people do stream a lot' (7.3.2016, personal interview). In 2019 this relationship is confirmed but the focus on TV 2 Play is increasing among the schedulers, and scheduling for the main channel is done in an interplay with the need to promote TV 2 Play (Holm Jensen, 9.4. 2019, personal interview). The head of scheduling at TV 2, Mette Rysø Johansen, strongly supports this understanding of how the relationship has evolved since 2016 (23.2.2016; 23.4.2019, personal interviews). However, scheduling still has to ensure that the flow of the audience's attention is directed towards using the content at the main channel, and the interplay between the social media, the tv2. dk website as well as TV 2 Play is paramount in order to achieve this goal. The strategy is conceptualised as a 'food chain' in the organisation (Rysø Johansen, 7.3.2016, personal interview) that aims to feed the top animal. Furthermore, the importance of the main channel seems to be growing as a promotional tool. Instead of just using trailers in the linear flow of the main channel, the promotional strategy appropriates social media together with the streaming service. An important early example of this strategy that seems to be setting the standard for the current work among the producers was the promotion of the documentary serial on poverty in Denmark: *På Røven i Nakskov* [*Broke in Nakskov*; Nakskov is a small town on the Danish island of Lolland] in April 2015. The first episode of the series was broadcast on the main channel on 23 April. Two weeks ahead of the premiere, trailers for the series had been shown on the main channel and the TV 2 website, after which they were picked up by a Facebook group of inhabitants and politicians from Lolland who began discussing the way their hometown was portrayed by TV 2. In the week before the premiere the first episode was given a preview on TV 2 Play. This generated a good deal of debate on the programme in the news media leading up to the premiere. After the broadcast, TV 2 mentioned the programme in the news and on the website, and the second episode was given a preview on TV 2 Play while the first was still available.

The case of *På Røven i Nakskov* prompted a new ecosystem approach to the TV 2 portfolio, the use of social media as promotional tools and the rather traditional focus on the linear main channel are financial first and political second. The audience for the main channel has been dwindling since 2007 but seems to have stabilised around a share of 25 per cent. Thus, securing this position has become the important focus of the producers. The commercial and political value of the market share has, however, become a weaker currency in the television industry because of the general decline in linear television use in prime time, especially among the commercially important target group: 20–40-year-old. Increasingly, the harder currency for the main channel is the extent of its reach of 85–90 per cent of Danes within a week. At the same time, securing this position of the main channel has become much more demanding and complicated in the present television market. The first lesson learned and added to the toolbox of the producers is that the workflow of promoting content has changed and is changing in new and still unpredictable ways. According to Mette Rysø Johansen, the producers are still in the process of understanding what the new logics of the promotional tactics they need to use are in order to 'find' the audience and guide them towards the main channel. In order to promote content, as the *På Røven i Nakskov* example above indicates, the emphasis on the main channel has in fact grown since 2016:

> Now, more than ever, the company should be happy to have a main channel. It plays an all-important role in order to make a well-functioning ecosystem work because it is able to attract large

audiences as well as being the 'place' from where audiences are directed to the other regions of the ecosystem and, most importantly, to TV 2 Play.

(Head of Scheduling Mette Rysø Johansen,
23.4.2019, personal interview)

These changes entail an emphasis on extensive coordination, cooperation and communication between the different divisions at TV 2. This work is very dependent on the analysis of the audience and the user behaviour based on Kantar Gallup's new television ratings measurement system presented in Chapter 2. As described the data consolidate live viewing and time shifted use of content until seven days after it is aired. The kind of knowledge about the audience these data provides is still the main source at TV 2. Furthermore, the interstitials have become promotional texts on other media. This means that a new kind quality demand has been added: the interstitials for high profile programmes need to be able to offer stand-alone entertainment value on, e.g. YouTube and Facebook, as well as promoting the programmes on the main channel and on the streaming service. An early example is the promotional campaign for the Tour de France 2015. The campaign consisted of four videos featuring situations from everyday life in Danish gardens in the summertime: a father and a son barbecuing sausages; a man watering flowers, and on purpose his wife gets a bit of water too; a man sleeping in a deck chair and a pregnant woman moving a parasol. The sound track in these rather uneventful videos was taken from the coverage of the Tour de France featuring TV 2's very famous team (in Denmark) of commentators evaluating the riders' performances.[2] The clash between what was seen and heard gave these trailers a sweet humorous quality.

In line with the need for stand-alone entertaining qualities the creative demands on the in-house production of promotional material and on the television production companies delivering parts of the material for this promotional ecosystem are increasing. At the same time the top-down management of the preproduction process of the on-air schedule has an increased influence on the editorial processes in the production of the different programmes. These production processes need to be managed much closer in order to deliver promotional material which is *usable* for this cross-media promotional system supporting the main channel. The on-air scheduling and marketing have to be included in the programme production process on a much earlier stage compared to the time when television was a stand-alone platform. It limits the autonomy of the commissioning editors and production companies a bit, and shifts the balance of power inside TV 2 as an organisation towards increased desktop management of the creative processes. An early example of this trend is the promotion of the fourth season of the very popular Danish dramedy serial *Badehotellet* (2013+) [The Seaside Hotel]. The production company (SF Film Production) had to produce special segments to be used for promotional purposes on social media, tv2.dk and linear television long before the editing process of the latest season was finished. The need for this kind of promotional material, bordering on actual programmes, is now a part of the commissioning of programmes from the independent producers. This material can also be used on TV 2 Play (Head of Scheduling Mette Rysø Johansen, 7.3.2016 and 23.4. 2019, personal interviews).

A second development that makes scheduling even more important has to do with the increasing promotional needs at TV 2 because of the non-linear use of television and the large portfolio of channels and services. According to Maria Gry Henriksen, former Head of Media and Development, it is no longer enough for a trailer to generate viewers for the first episode of a show. The viewers have to be reminded and guided much harder in order to return to watch the second episode of a show, and so forth. At the same time, the room for trailers on the main channel is very limited because the time available for promotion in the on-air schedule is taken up by the commercial breaks and an increasing number of sponsorship announcements. In short, *time scarcity* is a huge problem on the linear main channel. This means that the promotional campaigns have to be carefully selected and planned. The ability of a promotional campaign to generate viewers for the channels is measured by audience ratings, just like the programmes proper and the commercials. For instance, interstitials (such as trailers) have to meet estimated forecasts (for instance their reach in relation to the target group in question), and the flow planners do the daily editing of the schedule in *What's On* in order to meet these forecasts. There are also measurements of whether trailers actually result in viewers watching the programmes.

The second lesson: understanding the interplay of broadcasts and streaming

As described above, the role of the streaming service is primarily, and for the moment, to help secure the position of the 'top animal' in the ecosystem because of the traditional business model of commercially funded television. This is undoubtedly where the big money in the television industry still is, and the challenge facing producers involves protecting and supporting the financial flow as well as following the new habits of viewers. TV 2 Play is, however and at the same time, regarded as important in its own right in order to meet the increased non-linear use of television especially among the younger segments of the audience, and Chapter 6 will explore this in detail. The status and position of the streaming service in the TV 2-organisation are growing rapidly. I started the analysis of how the schedule and scheduling developed in 2014. Back then the management considered the streaming service a catch-up service. During 2016 the managerial focus turned towards supporting the interplay between the main channel and the streaming platform. At the end of 2018 strengthening the streaming service became the focus according to the company strategy (Boysen 2018). However, the changes to the organisational structure of the TV 2 company in January 2019 speak to the importance of the streaming service. The editorial teams of TV 2 Play and the youth channel TV 2 Zulu, as well as the scheduling of TV 2 Play, became part of a new division: *TV 2 Play Content*, along with the acquisition unit. The aim was to focus on strengthening the content for a young audience. Second, scheduling for the different channels in TV 2's portfolio was consolidated into one division, with a focus on securing content for TV 2 Play, and this change was mirroring changes in the commissioning process at TV 2. Teams based on genres were taking over from teams focussing on the individual channels, and a news desk for TV 2 Play was set up (Head of TV 2 Play Content Sune Roland, 9.4.2019, personal interview; Reseke 2019).

Even if the status of the streaming service is growing the revenue from the streaming service is still small compared with the revenue from the six linear channels, and especially the main channel. Furthermore, TV 2 does not have the amount of content and the financial muscle to produce enough new content to support a stand-alone streaming service like Netflix. This means that almost 90 per cent of the scheduling work is still aimed at making the main channel as strong as possible. The way the producers embrace the streaming service is by trying to deduce the logics of the interplay between the main channel and streaming in order to refute the decline in viewing time, particularly among the 20–40-year-olds in prime time. So far five sub-lessons have been learned about this interplay-based data included in the Kantar Gallup television ratings and additional user data from the streaming service:

1   Specific genres do well in this interplay and lead to better ratings and more users and time spent on both platforms: Danish language TV fiction and human-interest documentaries including

true crime (series and serials) are at the top of the pile. These top raking genres are flowed closely by reality game shows governed by what the head of scheduling calls 'TV 2 values' (Mette Rysø Johansen, 23.4.2019, personal interview). The hypothesis is that all profit from a 'water cooler' and an agenda setting effect among the audience and catch-ups and previews available on TV 2 Play stimulate this cooperation. The viewers are able to access the shows in many different ways, and being part of the public nature of television as a cultural forum is still very important. Furthermore, the narrative and aesthetic characteristic and thematic profiles of the programmes doing well are being explored in order to deduce common traits. At the moment factual programmes featuring and examining powerful human relations and personalities seem to be the common denominator. These genres are given high priority in the commissioning process.

2   Series of 6–10 episodes, factual as well as fiction, support ratings on both platforms as well, and are able to attract subscribers to TV 2 Play.

3   Placing entire Danish drama series that stimulate binging behaviour among the viewers is not good for neither the linear ratings nor user ratings at TV 2 Play. The hypothesis is that such drama series block the qualities described above, and do not encourage continued subscription to the streaming service.

4   Stacking – which is needed to support binge viewing across genres – is not a profitable scheduling tactic for a broadcaster with limits to new content as opposed to a global streaming service like Netflix. The backlist is much too small, and the content also has to feed the six linear channels.

5   Programme titles become increasingly important as a promotional paratextual tool for the streaming service as well as on the linear platform (Gray 2010; Ellis 2011). This is part of the overall drive towards the importance of the promotional material produced for the on-air schedule. The hypothesis is that it is becoming harder to capture the attention of the audience, and the way programmes are chosen is dependent on their ability to stand out on the linear and non-linear platforms among competing products. An example is the documentary *Gutterne på Kutterne* (2018) [The Lads on the Cutters, in Danish an alliteration is involved] and the lifestyle documentary *Min Sindssygt Sunde Familie* (2019) [My Insanely Healthy Family, an oxymoron and in Danish alliteration in involved] as well as *På Røven i Nakskov* described above. According to the producers these titles were provocative yet effective.

These sub-lessons on synergy are included in the schedulers' toolbox along with the existing tactics already in use (Eastman and Ferguson 2013). The aim at TV 2 is to understand this interplay in much more detail, and an important consequence of the sub-lessons learned so far is that in 2018 the need for content able to perform on both platforms led to a restructuring of the primetime schedule at the main channel. The second news cast at 10 pm was moved to 9:30 pm in order to reduce the number of primetime slots from three to two. The aim is to use the same amount of limited production resources on fewer programmes. Furthermore, all the schedulers interviewed in 2016 and 2019 acknowledge that two modes of watching television are used even if time shifting is possible, which is supported by the fact that 50 per cent of how TV 2 Play is used is for live streaming linear television. As a consequence, genres that do well on linear television are still given high priority, e.g. *Dancing with the Stars*, the news casts and morning talk shows.

The third lesson: branding the provider-viewer relationship

The third lesson regarding how to support the main channel centres on the stylistic and emotional dimension of the on-air schedule. The overall task involves working the identities of the different channels and platforms into a single 'brand' with the main channel as the 'mother ship' (Johnson 2012). At TV 2 the audio-visual design template for this work on a daily basis is the digital channel branding system *Miranda*. However, the time available in the on-air schedule to promote this provider identity is scarce. This means that the tools in the toolbox of the producers at TV 2 are being cultivated. In this process, the identity profile and fundamental values associated with TV 2 as a provider of public service television in Denmark play an important role for the producers, and especially the inherited *egalitarian values* associated with the TV 2 brand seem important to the production culture. In Chapter 3 these values were part of the identity branding interstitials used in the on-air-schedule, and in the following section the two major ways in which the producers interpret this legacy are presented.

The mirroring of identities – the audience as a cultural category

An important part of the provider's brand and heritage compared with DR and the commercial providers Nordic Entertainment Group (NENT) and Discovery is the notion that the viewers are heterogeneous, with regional and local cultural identities, in line with the provincial identity of TV 2. Espinosa (1982) terms this conceptualisation of the audience the 'cultural category' (ibid.: 85). As elaborated in Chapter 2 the audience is, in this sense, embedded in the television products, because the whole production process behind the final product is informed by this kind of professional knowledge held by individuals and the specific production culture and the final products. This conceptualisation taps into a discourse at TV 2 of cultural-political differences between the capital and provinces, and between urban and more rural life in Denmark. Moreover, the provider's brand identity has also supported the notion that the viewers share a homogeneous socio-cultural identity: we are all Danes, and this is in line with the main channel identity, where national and cultural cohesion across differences is underscored. The promotion of these inherited brand values of TV 2 as a public service provider, 'its DNA' (Head of TV 2, Lotte Lindegaard, at *Copenhagen Television Festival* on 18–19 August 2016), has become more important. The stylistic/aesthetic dimension of the on-air schedule is perceived as being increasingly important in order to enhance the provider-viewer relationship, and counter to the trend towards on-demand access to programmes the communicative qualities of live-ness, immediacy and sociability associated with the experience of watching traditional, linear television are given priority.

First, the producers have been experimenting with user-generated content in the on-air schedule (promotion producer Ole Sort, 31.5. 2016, personal interview). One very successful tool is the snippets of user-generated content described in Chapter 3. The viewers upload videos of their daily lives, and on the site, it is possible to view the video clips uploaded by others. Some of these videos will be used as interstitials leading into and out of the commercial breaks in the on-air schedule. These snippets show real situations from the everyday lives of ordinary Danes, and contain cute emotional situations such as children having fun or family pets performing tricks and the use of Danish traditions in connection with religious or seasonal holidays. Each snippet is provided with information on the identity of the people in the videos, and where in Denmark they live. The aesthetic qualities looked for in these snippets are what the promotion producer Ole Sort describes as 'something Granny could have filmed with her smartphone' (31.5. 2016, personal interview). Presently, this kind of 'instant aesthetics' (former Head of on-air Promotion Henrik Sand, 31.5. 2016, personal interview), and the authenticity it might produce, is considered important to the brand identity of TV 2 because of the existence of social media, smartphone cameras and the huge amount of audio-visual material produced by non-professionals. This strategy of including the viewer in the construction of on-air schedule may also serve to bridge the gap between the commercial and the editorial dimension of the on-air schedule at TV 2. As promotion producer Ole Sort puts it 'TV 2 can also be something the viewers have filmed themselves' (personal interview, 31.5. 2016). As elaborated in Chapter 3 the theme and aesthetics of the channel identity campaign *All that we share* running since 2017 are also part of this discourse of a shared identity across differences and of sociability.[3]

A second way to promote the provider-viewer relationship involves ongoing discussions of how to use the channel voice. For many years, the channel voice was a live production at TV 2, but is now recorded. The reason for this is the increasing time scarcity between the programmes, and live voices have a built-in unpredictability factor that the time frame and the playlist do not allow anymore. For example, a verbal mistake, a cough or a change in the speech tempo may use precious time that will seriously disturb the playlist. However, in 2016 the then head of on-air promotion, Henrik Sand, was considering going back to using live voices during prime time on the main channel. The kind of para-social communication, feeling of human presence and immediacy provided by the live channel voice is regarded as increasingly important to secure the attention of the viewers and the kind of 'personality' the TV 2 brand is promoting. The recorded channel voice leaves a somewhat artificial and mechanical impression according to Sand, and his point of view was supported by the continuity producers Stephan Randahl and Britt Lange (8.6. 2016, personal interviews).

Scheduling: first and last creative act

As this analysis has hopefully substantiated the tensions between the traditional well-known linear television environment and the non-linear services included in TV 2's portfolio are changing the production culture in ways that make on-air scheduling a far more complicated but also more important part of producing television. As Ellis has stated (2000b) scheduling is perhaps the last creative act in television, and I would add increasingly also the first. The producers all struggle to understand what on-air scheduling requires in order to secure the economic and political survival of the TV 2 company. At TV 2 this means that the aim is to ensure the survival of the main channel within the framework of the public service obligation and the media regulations in Denmark, as well as to meet the changing viewer habits. Even though the producers underscore the importance of online services in the portfolio, it is the genre schema of the traditional linear television schedule that seem to dominate the production culture even if change and adjustments are included. The driving force in this process of adaption is the dominant business model of the linear television paradigm: the commercial break, and it has a very strong conservative effect on the production culture. As a consequence, the conceptualisation of television in the production culture is still dominated by flow television's way of being part of the time structures of everyday life, serving as a public-private arena, which is supposed to attract an audience of scale. The task facing producers involves understanding and optimising the way in which the streaming service, the niche channels and the strategic use of social media can support this aim in new ways.

Across the three lessons learned to achieve this aim the production culture is changing. First and foremost, the workflow of promoting content and the demands on the qualities of the promotional material have changed. This entails a strengthened desktop organisational structure at TV 2 increasing the editorial power of the schedulers and on-air continuity producers in the creative processes. This enhancement is supported by the organisational changes taking place at TV 2 in 2019 with an emphasis on the integrated role of the streaming service in attracting an audience of scale. The development mirrors in many ways the development in the television industry in the 1990s as described in Chapter 1 when a competitive television market and the proliferation of channels also made organisational changes necessary in the public service companies and scheduling became paramount as a competitive tool (Ellis 2000a; Ytreberg 2002; Søndergaard 2003). Second, an understanding of the interplay between flow and SVOD scheduling is slowly emerging that is able to support both platforms. Certain genres stand out, the scheduling tactics are revised and the promotional value of the para-texts and trailers is getting more important. And third, a renewed focus is put on branding the viewer-provider relationship. New and older tools in the toolbox are being cultivated and dusted off for reconsideration in order to emphasise what are regarded the core values of the TV 2 brand: the egalitarian values. The need for promoting the provider identity and its communicative ethos is on the increase, and it must be able to entertain and attract the audience inside as well as outside the linear flow in an effort to 'find' and guide the viewers into profitable user flows. In this way, the spatial dimension in creating the textual structure and content leading to a 'flow' experience among the viewers is becoming more important for the producers. The same goes for the aesthetic/stylistic dimension of the 'flow' experience. The need for a strong and easily identifiable brand as a navigation tool is underscored. This is of huge importance on the provider level as well as on the channel and programme level (Johnson 2012). Furthermore, a personality level might be added to these levels of branding: providers as identifiable personalities in a crowded marketplace for audio-visual content.

To sum up, the producers of the on-air schedule are in this way an increasingly important part of the 'above the line' creative staff (Caldwell 2008), even if they mainly consider themselves as part of 'the engine room' of television production, as described above. As Ellis has pointed out (2000b) based on the changes to television in the 1980s and 1990s in Europe, scheduling is indeed a creative act. However, navigating the tensions between the two television paradigms seems to produce a kind of television where the linear and the non-linear seem to be integrated in the industry's practices as pointed out by Johnson (2017, 2019). These production cultures need to be followed in more detail and the way in which their practices are evolving may reveal a good deal about what television as a technology and a cultural form is, or is becoming, in the digital era. The next chapter in this book contributes to this work.

Notes

1 All quotes are translated from Danish by the author.
2 The videos are available at: www.youtube.com/watch?v=AJcoY5ClihA
3 The videos are available at: www.youtube.com/watch?v=jD8tjhVOlTc
  And at: www.youtube.com/watch?v=UQ15cqP-K80

References

Boysen, M. (2018) Ny organisering styrker TV 2. *TV 2 Newsletter*, 6 December. Available at https://omtv2.tv2.dk/nyhedsartikler/nyhedsvisning/ny-organisering-styrker-tv-2-play/

Caldwell, J. T. (2008) *Production Culture. Industrial Reflexivity and Critical Practice in Film and Television*. Durham: Duke University Press.

Eastman, S. T. and Ferguson, D. A. (2013) *Media Programming. Strategies & Practises*. Boston: Wadsworth Cengage Learning.

Ellis, J. (2011) Interstitials: How the 'Bits in Between' Define the Programmes. In P Grainge (ed.) *Ephemeral Media. Transitory Screen Culture from Television to YouTube*. London: Palgrave, pp. 59–69.

Ellis, J. (2000a) *Seeing Things. Television in the Age of Uncertainty*. London: I.B. Tauris Publishers.

Ellis, J. (2000b) Scheduling: The Last Creative Act in Television? *Media, Culture and Society*, 22(1), pp. 25–38.

Espinosa, P. (1982) The Audience in the Text: Ethnographic Observations of a Hollywood Story Conference. *Media, Culture & Society*, 4 (1), pp. 77–86.

Gray, J. (2010) *Shows Sold Separately. Promos, Spoilers, and Other Media Paratexts.* New York: New York University Press.

Johnson, C. (2019) *Online TV.* London: Routledge.

Johnson, C. (2017) Beyond Catch-up: VoD Interfaces, ITV Hub and the Repositioning of Television Online. *Critical Studies in Television*, 12(2), pp. 121–138.

Johnson, C. (2012) *Branding Television.* London: Routledge.

Reseke, L. (2019) TV 2 Nyhederne opretter ny redaktion til Play og skruer på bemandingen. *MediaWatch*, 27 February. Available at https://mediawatch.dk/secure/Medienyt/TV/article11218444.ece

Søndergaard, H. (2003) Programfladestyring og organisationsforandringer i nordiske public service-fjernsyn. *Mediekultur*, 35, pp. 5–23.

TV 2 Public service redegørelse 2018 (2019) Odense: TV 2 Danmark A/S.

TV 2 årsrapport 2018 (2019) Odense: TV 2 Danmark A/S.

Van Den Bulck, H. and Enli, G. S. (2014a) Flow Under Pressure: Television Scheduling and Continuity Techniques as Victims of Media Convergence? *Television and New Media*, 15(5), pp. 441–452.

Van Den Bulck, H. and Enli, G. S. (2014b) Bye, Bye "Hello Ladies?": In-Vision Announcers as Continuity Technique in a European Post Linear Television Landscape: The Case of Flanders and Norway. *Television and New Media*, 15(5), pp. 453–469.

Ytreberg, E. (2002) Continuity in Environments. The Evolution of Basic Practices and Dilemmas in Nordic Television Scheduling. *European Journal of Communication*, 17(3), pp. 283–304.

6 Dilemmas in multi-platform scheduling

Introduction

An important dimension of scheduling traditional, linear television is making scarce resources go a long way, and in an industry where the need for new content and content turnover is very high (Eastman and Ferguson 2013: 21–22), scheduling is typically marked by an overarching frugality. The challenge is to repurpose content in different ways, in order to fill a growing number of outlets in ways that make them attractive to the viewers. This need to repurpose content holds a number of dilemmas for the producers in their interpretation of their work in the current tensions between linear and the non-linear scheduling. The chapter continues the analysis in Chapter 5 of how the production culture adapts at the public service company, TV 2. It focusses specifically on the dilemmas the producers face when the aim is to schedule the TV 2 Play streaming service in a way that appeals to a young audience and retains the subscribers. A simultaneous aim is to schedule the linear niche channel, TV 2 Zulu, with a target group of 15–39-year-olds and a viewing share of 1.7 per cent, in a way that retains the viewers and keeps Zulu alive as a linear channel. There are only around 1.8 million individuals in this age group in the Danish population of 5.6 million; however, this target group is an institutionally important segment of the audience (Ettema and Whitney 1994).

To recapitulate, TV 2 Zulu is part of TV 2's commercial division TV 2 Networks, just as TV 2 Play is. All TV 2's channels are funded by commercials and subscriptions, except for its regional network of eight affiliated companies that are supported by a share of the public funding for public service media and content production in Denmark. Subscriptions to bundles of linear channels distributed by the cable companies and the operator of the Danish digital terrestrial television network are of paramount importance for securing a revenue and the stability of TV 2's business model. 54 per cent of the company's revenue comes from subscriptions (*TV 2 Årsrapport 2018* 2019), and TV 2's streaming service contributes to this source of commercial revenue. The main channel has a public service obligation and it is the company's economic mothership, as elaborated in Chapters 3 and 5, and the state ownership of the limited company that make the company define its identity as a publicist rather than a commercial company. A key concern is that the schedulers' work is defined by limited resources, and similar to the findings in Chapter 5 this means that the linear television paradigm is still a very strong influence on the production culture. As pointed out by Andersen, this situation entails what could be termed a 'broadcastification' (Andersen 2017: 84) of the steaming service. However, it also confronts the traditional strategic practices and tactics of scheduling with three major dilemmas that show that it is much harder to do cross-platform scheduling when it comes to a young and very small target group in a small market compared to a mainstream audience of some scale.

Organisational change and the young audience

As elaborated in Chapter 5, the status and position of the TV 2 organisation's streaming service are growing rapidly. The January 2019 changes to the organisational structure of the TV 2 company speak to the importance of the streaming service. The editorial teams of TV 2 Play and TV 2 Zulu's editorial teams became part of the same new unit: *TV 2 Play Content*. The aim was to strengthen content commissioning for a young audience, and the TV 2 Play 'brand.' Second, scheduling for TV 2 Play and the various channels of TV 2's portfolio was consolidated into one division that focussed on securing content for TV 2 Play, and this change mirrored changes in the commissioning process at TV 2. The editorial teams were based on genres, rather than focussed on the individual channels, and a news desk for TV 2 Play was set up too (Boysen 2018; Reseke 2019).

Even if TV 2 is trying to focus on its streaming service and to strengthen its position, the linear youth channel is, nevertheless, not dispensable. For now (2019), TV 2 will not follow in the footsteps of DR, which will make its youth channel, DR3, into an online-only channel in 2020, just as the BBC did with BBC3 in 2016. TV 2 still needs to make money on all platforms, and TV 2 Zulu has a 1.7 per cent share of the viewing audience, and the youngest audience among the channels for adults on the Danish market. Average age is 39 years. However, its target group is increasingly difficult to attract. First, household penetration is a growing problem for TV 2 Zulu. Since 2015, the channel is no longer part of the most used television channel bundle delivered by the cable and telecom company YouSee, and penetration dropped from about 65 per cent in 2013 to 42.6 per cent in 2018 (*TV 2 Årsrapport 2018* 2019: 13). Second, TV 2 Zulu's target group is among the audience segments with the fastest-changing viewing habits. The time that 19–34-year-olds spent watching television dropped from two hours a day in 2010 to one hour and nine minutes in 2018 (Agency for Culture and Palaces, *Mediernes Udvikling i Danmark: TV og Streaming* 2019: 17), and commercial television has been especially hit by this trend. In Denmark, commercial television channels used to have a strong hold on the younger segments thanks to a programming profile of American television series and films. This profile is no longer competitive because of the streaming services now available, and these services' genre profiles (Agency for Culture and Palaces, *Mediernes Udvikling i Danmark: Streaming* 2018: 10). TV 2 Zulu's target group belongs to a group of viewers that tends to replace a lot of traditional television viewing with streaming, for example, 68 per cent of 19–34-year-olds stream every day (Agency for Culture and Palaces, *Mediernes Udvikling i Danmark: Streaming* 2018: 12), 51 per cent watch Netflix every day, and 49 per cent watch YouTube every day (ibid: 21). Furthermore, even if the viewing share of the channel's target group is relatively stable, the ratings are dropping, and this means that the commercial value of the channel is weakening. To counterbalance the decline in viewership, the use of the content produced for TV 2 Zulu on TV 2 Play is important. A 2016 in-house report states that [then] 71 per cent of TV 2 Play subscribers had started to watch TV 2 Zulu content during the first six months of 2015 (Nilausen 2016: 24). Furthermore, a 2018 in-house report states that content for TV 2 Zulu is responsible for 22 per cent of the overall VOD-uses of TV 2 content (Bruhn Hansen and Bock Jeppesen 2018: 22). TV 2 Play's target group is the 20–60-year-olds, and although it is a bit older, it also overlaps Zulu's. The service has around 500.000 subscribers (August 2019) and among SVODs on the Danish market, TV 2 Play is number three, after Netflix and ViaPlay (Agency of Culture and Palaces, *Mediernes Udvikling i Danmark: Streaming* 2018: 18).

The circumstances described above mean that the schedulers face new challenges and dilemmas when the aim is to make content go as far as possible. First, the rationale of the many types of reruns on linear television is questioned. As a tool, the rerun is probably losing its rationale in the current television developments, along with the many tactics of shuffling content in the linear schedule in order to cover a 24/7 broadcast schedule. Second, these problems indicate the growing need for fresh releases of high-end material, or 'prized content,' as Amanda Lotz terms the kind of content that the viewers 'seek out and specifically desire' (Lotz 2014: 12). This kind of content may be added to a back-catalogue, to avoid churn rates to grow among the subscribers. In the following part of this chapter, I present three dilemmas facing the practices of the schedulers that have to cater to both platforms. My analysis is based on downloads of broadcasting plans and screen dumps of TV 2 Zulu's schedules for week 46 of 2018, and weeks 11–12 of 2019. These weeks belong to the A- and C-schedules following the high seasons for television viewing in Denmark. Data from my own analysis in Kantar Gallup's *TV Viewing database* and screen shots of TV 2 Play's interface for week 46 of 2018 and weeks 11–12 of 2019 are used for the analysis and it focusses on the front page of the streaming service. I have used my own premium subscription to TV 2 Play. Compared to the basic subscription models, the premium model includes access to all the linear channels in the portfolio (including the commercial breaks between the programmes), no commercials as preview, and a selection of films. The analysis also builds on trade press contributions and on in-house and public TV 2 documents. Finally, it builds on personal interviews and written correspondence from the spring of 2019, with head of content for TV 2 Play and TV 2 Zulu Sune Roland, head of TV 2 Play Kurt Holm Jensen, media planner Mikkel Andersen and head of scheduling Mette Rysø Johansen.

Availability meets reruns

The first dilemma facing scheduling for the target group of 15–39-year-olds is that the availability of prized content on TV 2 Play has to follow a *different temporal strategy* than that used for linear scheduling for TV 2 Zulu. However, TV 2 Play is a highly edited service in a dynamic and close interplay with the linear channels. The service has a limited amount of content that is produced for this service only, and TV 2 Play serves as a showroom that is furnished with content that is considered prized content, harvested from the various linear channels in the company's portfolio. It carries TV 2's Danish language productions, almost no foreign acquisition, and the series promoted are the most popular ones on linear television, with known or, in the case of new content, assumed appeal to the young audience segments. This means that content produced for TV 2 Zulu's target group occupies a very prominent position. To retain the subscribers and to attract new ones, the service needs to stretch new series of prized content over the entire year. The strategy implemented since 2019 is called PLAY52 and/or PLAY365, and aims to ensure that the streaming service does not lose subscribers during off-season periods of traditional television scheduling. Blocks of this kind of attractive content also have to follow each other, and avoid huge overlaps, in order to cover all 365 days during 52 weeks. This means that when a popular series comes to its final episodes, it is crucial to make new, similar-quality content available. To make this work, the scheduling at TV 2 Play in fact has to avoid mirroring the way the linear channels are scheduled in seasons, following various distribution plans. Linear television is scheduled in seasons, where the popular series and the new material are scheduled in two big waves. In Denmark, the A-plan and the C-plan are the industry terms for the two periods where prized content is bundled and stacked in prime time, and these periods have very high commercial value to the company. During the summer months, from June until September, the B-plan takes over. It is part of industry lore that Danes do not watch much television during the summer. This raises a 'chicken or egg' question, because historically, the low priority given to the summer months has been a way to save content resources, as the schedules are full of reruns and foreign acquisitions, and no new content is broadcast. The result of these production practices is that television viewing drops dramatically during these months and traditional scheduling strategies create a huge problem for the streaming service:

> The subscribers are streaming out of the 'shop' [TV 2 Play] when the high season of television ends. This is in fact not a kind of pattern you can allow when you run a streaming service. TV 2 Play needs to offer attractive content during the summer months.
>
> (Head of TV 2 Play Content Sune Roland,
> personal interview, 9.4.2019)

According to the producers, the foregoing pattern is a huge problem for the streaming service in two interconnected ways. First, the churn rate grows during these months, with no *new* prized content available on TV 2 Play. This is partly because it is very easy to cancel the subscription, and if nothing new is available and you have watched the content you wanted, users tend to cancel their subscription. Second, the churn rate also grows when there is no *new* prized content available on TV 2 Zulu. It is not however that easy to cancel a linear channel that is part of a bundle provided by the cable and telecom companies. Nevertheless, the lack of new content does not support the penetration of TV 2 Zulu either but adds to this problem. The dilemma is that these acknowledged temporal needs and synergies between the streaming platform and TV 2 Zulu clash significantly with the linear delay economy, elaborated in Chapter 4, that governs the scheduling practices of the niche channel. First and foremost, the linear channel has a very limited amount of first-run, prized content during the weeks of the A-plan season. For example, during 12–18 November 2018 only five hours of 168 were first-run content, and not all these first-runs were prized content, even if they were broadcast in a prime-time slot: for example, one hour and ten minutes were spent on the British *XFactor*. From 14 to 21 March 2019 there were only two hours and 55 minutes of first-run content, comprising five 20-minute episodes of *Family Guy*.

In comparison to this pattern at TV 2 Zulu, the curation of TV 2 Play seems to 'tentpole' the front page, and *no priority* is given to what Lotz calls 'linear content' (Lotz 2014: 14), which is the kind of programme to which viewers pay little attention, according to Lotz. In traditional linear scheduling, 'tentpoling' is a tool used to flag a channel's most important and/or successful programmes in a schedule otherwise filled with weaker content that has lower ratings (Eastman and Ferguson 2009). This kind of content is prominently placed in terms of its position and the amount of space it occupies in the layout. Figure 6.1 illustrates the layout of the interface, and this example is taken from Monday, 18 March 2019:

The horizontal rows of para-texts (Gray 2010) featuring the various programmes are called 'tiles,' whereas the vertical rows of para-texts are called 'decks,' and the schedulers import this terminology from computer interface design. On TV 2 Play's front page, the biggest tiles are in the top deck, which comprises a dynamic series of 6–11 programmes available in a so-called 'merry-go-round' that moves from left to right. This deck is equivalent to editorial top priority, and is changed every day of the week. There are 14 decks on the front page, and decks one to four are edited three times a day according to topicality, much like the front page of a print newspaper. Each of the 13 decks below the top deck may be scrolled horizontally and each tile may be clicked open for more programme choices vertically. Each deck has a heading, and at TV 2 Play these are relatively stable. The second deck (September 2019) is 'the editorial recommendation,' the third is 'start watching' and the fourth is 'popular right now.' According to the head of TV 2 Play Kurt Holm Jensen the allocation of position and space is based on various sources of knowledge about the viewing patterns on the service TV 2 Play. A key performance indicator (KPI) for measuring success is *Activated subscribers*, which is defined

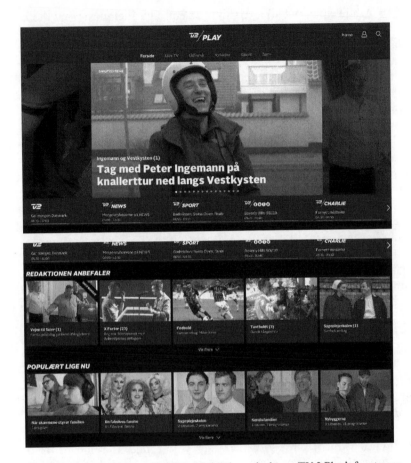

Figure 6.1 The 'merry-go-round' and the three decks on TV 2 Play's front page.

as a subscriber that has *activated* the content on the streaming service for some time, in a given time frame. TV 2 uses Adobe Analytics and key measurements are 1: video time: how much time is used, 2: content starts: how much content is stated in a given time period, and 3: video views: how much content is used. Second, the TV-ratings that include seven days of streaming are another hugely important source of information for the editorial gatekeeping, and finally, there is a pressing need to promote upcoming new content at TV 2.

  TV 2 Play tentpoles Danish-language fiction, and comedies are given special priority because they are the most popular genre on TV 2 Play, followed by Danish versions of reality formats (e.g. *XFactor, The*

Block), Danish-language, agenda-setting documentaries, lifestyle programming and sports events. In other words, in the Danish context, prized content cuts across the categories that fit 'the post-network' era argued by Lotz (2014: 12–16), and certainly runs counter to the content profiles of transnational streaming services such as Netflix, which promotes catalogues dominated by American content (Lobato 2019). In 2017, the European share of content in Netflix's 27 catalogues was 15 per cent, and the share of national content in the Danish catalogue was 1 per cent (Grece and Pumares 2017: 16–18). The language and the cultural context are the common denominators, rather than whether it is suited a live broadcast or may be viewed on-demand at any time. According to all the interviewees at TV 2 these genres not only attract new subscribers but also appeal to TV 2 Zulu's target group. However, the value of Danish-language comedies produced for a young audience tops the chart. The comedies, *Shit Happens*, *Perfect Places* and the hugely successful *Clown*, did extremely well with this target group, and such comedies are one of TV 2 Zulu's trademarks. They have great value to the channel brand, which is associated with entertainment, informal playfulness, pushing boundaries and creativity (Bruhn Hansen 2016: 33; Bruhn Hansen and Bock Jeppesen 2018: 17). On TV 2 Play, Danish-language television fiction is also the genre that best engages the subscribers. However, this is the most expensive genre to produce, and the question is whether TV 2 has the economy to produce many of these series for a very small segment of an audience that is increasingly leaving traditional television for its entertainment.

Currently, the company strives to broaden the scope of its genres, and the whole range of the prized content produced for TV 2 Zulu's target group has a prominent position. The aim is to promote the cheaper yet still popular genres, and the schedulers seem to rely on 'hammocking,' known from linear scheduling and used with a twist on the non-linear platform. The promotion of fresh series produced for TV 2 Zulu is placed on a tile in the merry-go-round between two already strong series in the target group. An example from Sunday 17 March 2019 is a preview of a new docusoap, *A Fabulous Family*, about the everyday lives of three drag queens, placed between two series with several seasons and high ratings, and an appeal to a young audience: the Danish version of *The Block* and the Danish quiz show *The Clip Fishermen*.

The curation of the top decks of the front-page attempts to create the impression of a continuous stream of newly available content, and the content on the decks is edited in a close interplay with the scheduling of the linear portfolio elaborated in Chapter 5. Preview – of either next episodes of a series or the first episodes of new series – is a very frequently used tool. As pointed out by Stewart (2016) and Johnson (2019: 115), streaming services aim to produce the illusion of a perpetually refreshed and huge catalogue that offers endless viewing choices, and this also applies to TV 2 Play. It is relatively easy to create this impression when producing the schedule for TV 2 Play, because it is rather difficult for the user to obtain an overview of the catalogue. This clashed significantly with the impression of 'nothing new' that TV 2 Zulu's scheduling practices easily suggest. To make content go as far as possible, intensive shuffling is used. As Andersen points out in his comprehensive analysis of TV 2 Zulu (2017), shuffling means that snap reruns of a new episode with the latest episodes of prized content are distributed horizontally during a period of time, to gather an audience and fill the schedule. An example is the way the stand-up comedy programme, *Dybvaaaad*, was used from 12 to 18 November 2018: episode 10 of the new 2018 season of *Dybvaaaad* broadcasts during prime time on 12 November, and leading in is episode 9 in a snap rerun from last week. Early in the morning that day, three episodes from the 2014 season were aired, and this season is continuously aired in this time slot the rest of the week, except Sunday. Then, a snap rerun of episode 10 was aired during prime time on Friday, and Saturday night too, with episode 9 as a lead-in, and finally episodes 9 and 10 were aired Sunday night between 3 and 4 am. However, the value of shuffling is declining at TV 2 Zulu, because TV 2 Play makes the content available ahead of the broadcast, in order to retain and attract the same target group. Also, frequent use of the tool makes the schedule stand out as a channel with almost no new content to watch.

The way TV 2 Play ignores channel brands in order to meet the goals of the PLAY52/365 strategy within limited resources adds to this impression of a linear channel with very little new content on offer. At TV 2 Play there is a need to schedule genres instead of channels, and Danish-language fiction is popular with all age groups. It needs to be promoted without associations to a specific channel that the young audience knows to have a programming profile aimed at another segment of the audience. An example from the two-week sample from 2019 is the second season of the Danish dramedy, *The Nursing School*, set in the 1950s and produced for the niche channel, TV 2 Charlie, with a target group of over 55-year-olds. To schedule TV 2 Play with no regard to the channel brands clashes with TV 2 Zulu's effort to create a clear channel brand that a young audience values highly. As the organisational changes at TV 2 already suggest, the genre-driven scheduling of TV 2 Play has ramifications for the entire way of commissioning content at TV 2, with various genres and the allocation of resources for these productions being prioritised.

Increased content demands meet limited resources

The scheduling of TV 2 Play demands more material attractive to the young audience segments, and to the target group of TV 2 Zulu, in order to meet the aims of PLAY52/365. This means more low-budget series with no fewer than 6–10 episodes are needed to generate a larger volume of new content to promote on both platforms. This is a general need for the streaming service and affects its interaction with all linear channels in the portfolio, not just TV 2 Zulu. However, because Zulu's target group is very small and difficult to attract, the investment of resources is an issue. To address this need with limited resources, TV 2 Play is filled with new content in three ways. First, new content is produced, which supports programmes that are already popular with the target group. An example is a series of 'behind the scenes' productions that follow the work of the three judges and the host of TV 2's version of *XFactor*. These are between 8 and 10 minutes long. Second, short items with no connection to the programmes on the linear channels are also produced. In 2018 and 2019 a series of documentaries called *ECHO* was produced, featuring one- to two-minute interviews with young Danes doing well in life, despite adverse personal circumstances. *Minidoks* is another example of this kind of experiment, and these series feature episodes between 6 and 20 minutes long, which reflect the agenda in the news media. All in all, the low-budget content produced for TV 2 Play has no value for the linear channel, because it does not fit a traditional time-slot structure.

To meet the aims of the PLAY52/365-strategy well-known scheduling tools are implemented to create the *impression of newness*, rather than making actual new content available. Again, *shuffling* is a tool used for scheduling the merry-go-round in the top deck of TV 2 Play on a daily basis. An example is the promotion of programmes on 14 and 15 March 2019: the programmes promoted are the same, but all programmes except one have another place in the merry-go-round, and the para-texts have been changed for two of the programmes. Another way to shuffle the same content is by moving the same programmes to the lower decks of the TV 2 Play's front page. In these decks, the *antology* scheduling tool is used, following the various headings mentioned above (Adams and Eastman 2013). This tool repositions the same content under different headings during the week. An example is the placement of the latest episode of *The Nursing School* under 'Popular now' as well as in the merry-go-round. To sum up, scheduling the steaming platform in this manner, with new programmes in the top decks, is aimed at supporting high ratings and the traditional business model at TV 2. Seven days after a linear broadcast, the use of the archived programmes available at TV 2 Play is not included in the metrics of television viewing, even if the on-demand service, in theory, supports a long tail.

A third frequently used scheduling tool at TV 2 Play that creates the impression of newness and abundance is *stacking*. This means that the latest season of a popular programme becomes available in its entirety when it has been broadcast on a linear channel, and the viewers are given access to the back-catalogue of seasons at the same time. Stacking seasons and sneak previews are like the delay economy with a twist, and tap into the emerging impatience-culture tendencies described in Chapter 4. The rationale behind withholding content that is already available is dwindling, and in effect the conceptualisation of the audience is changing. Nevertheless, this on-demand way of using the tool clashes with the delay economy of linear scheduling. In many ways these appropriations of content at TV 2 Play make TV 2 Zulu lose one of its most important scheduling tools in the struggle to make content go as far as possible, while the need to produce more expensive content to feed both TV 2 Zulu and TV 2 Play grows.

Interdependence

The third major dilemma facing the schedulers is the fundamental need for a two-platform strategy at TV 2. Even if the scheduling needs for TV 2 Zulu and TV 2 Play are very different and clash in many ways, dropping the linear channel is not an option at TV 2. As described above, the schedulers are aware of the fact that there seems to be a large degree of *interdependence* between the linear and the non-linear platforms. According to Kurt Holm Jensen, head of TV 2 Play, the cross-promotional value of TV 2 Zulu and the synergy between the two platforms are important to increasing subscriptions to the streaming platform:

> We are able to speak to the viewers' habits by making trailer campaigns for a TV 2 Zulu programme in the linear universe, and perhaps attract some new subscribers to TV 2 Play in this way. And among the channel 'shavers' who subscribe only to the main channel in the linear universe, we may get some to become subscribers to TV 2 Play, instead. The linear channels are a huge promotional engine that we have at TV 2, and we want to hang on to this, no matter what it takes. We need to closely coordinate the two when promoting new content in the schedules and on the streaming platform.
>
> (Head of TV 2 Play, Kurt Holm Jensen, personal interview, 23.4.2019)

Sune Roland, head of the new division TV 2 Play Content, strongly supports the need to apply the synergy between the two ways of watching television to scheduling, and this involves a better understanding of the qualities of specific programmes. An example is the recent, unexpected success of the Danish version of the Channel4 game show, *Naked Attraction* (2019), which did extremely well with the target group on both platforms.

At TV 2 Play, the content produced for TV 2 Zulu risks drowning, and therefore the linear channel dedicated to the target group is important, to retain the subscriptions to the television bundles that include TV 2 Zulu. 58 per cent of the content consists of American comedy and dramedy series (*TV 2 Public service rapport 2017* 2018: 27), and scheduling at TV 2 Zulu is dominated by stacking and stripping these series vertically and horizontally throughout the day- and night-parts of the schedule throughout the week, all year round. The content produced for TV 2 Zulu includes Danish stand-up comedy, comedy series, reality game shows and a few awards shows and events organised by the channel. These programmes are positioned in the channel's prime time between 9 and 11 pm, and reruns are typically stacked and stripped in this time slot throughout the week. A very predictable schedule is produced week after week, and it is possible for the viewers to generate an 'inner schedule.' All in all, this kind of scheduling suggests a low-budget television channel, and this may be one reason the ratings are dropping for this channel, and not only because of competition from streaming services and social media. Nevertheless, to reach a viewing share of about 1.7 per cent, this kind of scheduling is necessary, because it could never be achieved with the very small number of first-run, prime-time content alone. Instead, especially during the day, the channel attracts an audience by block scheduling well-known old American series such as *Beverly Hills 90210*, *Desperate Housewives* and *Friends*. An example is episode five of *Ugly Betty* from 2006, which aired Sunday 18 November 2018 at 10.30 am, and attracted a 5 per cent share of viewers. This channel seems to fit the everyday rhythms of a young audience, for example, watching television to relax, as moving wall paper, for getting over a hangover or for falling asleep. These series are not available on TV 2 Play, and in a sense, TV 2 Zulu acts as a channel for a back-catalogue of content that has to be aired according to acquisition contracts, but has little value to TV 2. But TV 2 Zulu also broadcasts genres that do really well on linear television: live transmissions from Zulu events and Zulu awards shows. However, this genre has little value to the linear channel's viewer share, because it has very limited rerun-value, and is relatively expensive to produce, even if the programmes get high ratings.

Conclusion: scheduling for whom?

To sum up, it is safe to say that conflicting needs and disruptive economic and communicative interdependence mark the production culture at TV 2 when it comes to cross-platform scheduling for niche channels in the portfolio. The need for prized content produced for a volatile, very small, yet important target group clashes with the need to keep the linear channel alive by stretching the tools and the practices of linear scheduling to a maximum, and perhaps beyond. Furthermore, as also noted by Andersen (2017) a 'broadcastification' of the streaming platform is applied when adapting scheduling strategies and tools from the linear television paradigm to the non-linear platform. Nevertheless, this adaptation is creating a growing problem for the TV 2 Zulu channel brand, otherwise known to attract the target group of 15–39-year-olds very effectively. However, the question is whether the way TV 2 Zulu is scheduled is a fruitful and sustainable approach that supports the synergy between the two platforms. It could be argued that the brand value of TV 2 Zulu is presently suffering or at the edge of having very little to do with the actual programming on the channel, and that the linear channel needs more prized content in order to play its part in securing economic and communicative interdependence. The number of reruns and the dominance of back-catalogue content seem problematic, if the aim is to promote the values associated with the channel's brand, as presented above. As pointed out, TV 2 Play's scheduling uses programmes, and not channels, as its guiding principle, and in this sense the focus on the Zulu brand disappears when the programmes are made available on TV 2 Play. Sune Roland, the head of TV 2 Play Content, acknowledges that this is a growing dilemma for the organisation:

> This is a huge discussion. Some companies are more prepared to discard the channels than we are. TV 2 will continue to emphasise the channels because we think the viewers actually like the edited and curated compilation that the channel will be able to offer.
> (Roland, personal interview, 9.4.2019)

A second concern related to the acknowledged and argued interdependence of the linear and the non-linear platforms important to the production culture is that TV 2 Play is unable to include the many communicative functions of the on-air schedule. However, the TV 2

Zulu brand is strongly associated with this third tier of the schedule as a televisual genre. Since the channel's launch in 2000, TV 2 Zulu has been particularly known for its innovative and humorous interstitials: the animated channel logos, an iconic channel voice and specific channel branding campaigns. An example of the kind of channel branding in question is the 2009 series, *The Hugging Team*. This series was made up of pranks that all feature a group of four men posing as members of the Hells Angels bikers, sent on a mission by a young man's best friends. Instead of beating up the young man, the four Hells Angels gave him a big hug, and subsequently the practical joke was revealed to the very scared young man.[1] This kind of dark humour that works against prejudices has been a TV 2 Zulu trademark for 20 years, and has developed a specific house style that is evident throughout the promotional texts in the on-air schedule and the programmes. Head of TV 2 Play Content regards this specific house style as a part of the provider–viewer relationship that is still extremely important to maintain (Roland 9.4.2019, personal interview). The question is whether this traditional communicative interface that caters to a special provider–user relationship is important to the viewers, and whether it plays a part in maintaining the synergies between the two platforms. The inherited frugality runs the risk of damaging TV 2 Zulu's possibilities as a 'subcultural forum' (Lotz 2014: 47) for a segment of the audience that is regarded as very important to the public service identity of the TV 2 company in the digital era.

All in all, the production culture at TV 2 is trying to adapt its practices, which create a situation where distinctions between linear and non-linear television paradigms do not really apply. Instead, the findings indicate a far more blurred development in the television industry. Johnson (2019: 127) defines this development in the television industry as 'online TV,' which is characterised by an integration of linear and the non-linear features. I argue that this integration of communicative features in the production of the schedule may be seen as an emerging third television paradigm produced by the adjusted practices in the production culture, in which industrial continuity is as important to consider as is change. The final chapter of this book elaborates these discussions and future trajectories of the television industry.

Note

1 An example of this channel identity-campaign is available at www.youtube.com/watch?v=gm7-gW4v7IE

References

Adams, W. J. and Eastman, S. T. (2013) Prime Time Network Programming Strategies. In S. T. Eastman and D. A. Ferguson (eds.) *Media Programming Strategies and Practices.* Boston: Wadsworth Cengage learning, pp. 45–90.

Agency for Culture and Palaces (2019) *Mediernes Udvikling i Danmark: TV og Streaming.* København: Slots- og Kulturstyrelsen.

Agency for Culture and Palaces (2018) *Mediernes Udvikling i Danmark: Streaming.* København: Slots- og Kulturstyrelsen.

Andersen, M. (2017) *Mellem lineært TV og On-demand. En undersøgelse af TV 2 Zulus scheduling på tværs af platform.* Unpublished master thesis, Aarhus University.

Boysen, M. (2018) Ny organisering styrker TV 2. *TV 2 Newsletter,* 6th December. Available at https://omtv2.tv2.dk/nyhedsartikler/nyhedsvisning/ny-organisering-styrker-tv-2-play/

Bruhn Hansen, A. S. (2016) *TV 2 Zulu Brandbog 2016 – viden til indsigt.* In-house document. Odense: TV 2.

Bruhn Hansen, A. S. and Bock Jeppesen, N. M. (2018) *TV 2 Zulu Brandbog 2018 – viden til indsigt.* In-house document. Odense: TV 2.

Eastman, S. T. and Ferguson, D. A. (2013) *Media Programming Strategies and Practices.* Boston: Wadsworth Cengage learning.

Eastman, S. T. and Ferguson, D. A. (2009) *Media Programming Strategies and Practices.* Boston: Wadsworth Cengage learning.

Ettema, J. S. and Whitney, D. C. (1994) The Money Arrow: An Introduction to Audiencemaking. In J. C. Ettema and D. C. Whitney (eds.) *Audiencemaking: How the Media Create the Audience.* London: Sage, pp. 1–18.

Gray, J. (2010) *Shows Sold Separately. Promos, Spoilers, and Other Media Paratexts.* New York: New York University Press.

Grece, C. And Pumares, M. J. (2017) *The Origin of TV Content in VOD Catalogues – 2017 Edition.* Strasbourg: European Audiovisual Observatory.

Johnson, C. (2019) *Online TV.* London: Routledge.

Lobato, R. (2019) *Netflix Nations. The Geography of Digital Distribution.* New York: New York University Press.

Lotz, A. (2014) *The Television Will Be Revolutionized.* New York: New York University Press.

Nilausen, A. (2016) *TV 2Play Brandbog 2016.* In-house document. Odense: TV 2.

Reseke, L. (2019) TV 2 Nyhederne opretter ny redaktion til Play og skruer på bemandingen. *MediaWatch,* 27 February. Available at https://mediawatch.dk/secure/Medienyt/TV/article11218444.ece

Stewart, M. (2016) The Myth of Televisual Ubiquity. *Television and New Media,* 17(8), pp. 691–707.

TV 2 Årsrapport 2018 (2019) Odense: TV 2 Danmark A/S.

7 Digital television

The book's focus on the schedule as a core genre of television and on scheduling as a professional practice in the television industry contributes with research findings to an important but strangely under-researched aspect of television in international television studies. It is part of a new wave of scheduling studies emerging in the wake of the competition for audiences facing the incumbent television industry from Over The Top (OTT)-companies like Netflix, HBO and Amazon Prime that was elaborated in Chapter 2. This new wave of academic interest continues the research on the developments in the pre-digital era of television competition in Europe during the 1990s. Back then the schedule and scheduling as a professional craft became an important tool in the growing competition in the television industry during this period as a result of the deregulation of the television systems in many European countries. As the chapters in this book show the skill of scheduling content for multi-platform portfolios has become more important, yet scheduling has also become much more complex and difficult. Audiences have gained enhanced control over what to watch, as well as when and where to watch television, and retaining and guiding the increasingly fragmented audience towards profitable user flows have therefore become a challenge across commercial and public service television. In Europe and especially in the Nordic countries public service television is of huge cultural-political importance to the incumbent television industry and connected to the special cultural-political needs of countries with small populations and languages (Syvertsen et al. 2014). In this kind of dual television-system the tensions between the traditional linear television paradigm and the emerging non-linear paradigm have a growing influence on the schedule as the communicative interface between the different broadcasters and the implied viewers, and it has an influence on the production culture producing it. As argued in Chapter 1 of this book the schedule

consists of three tiers and it performs five important functions fundamental to the industry and to the communicative relationship between
the television company and the viewers. In Chapter 2 I argued that this
televisual and textual phenomenon is a core genre of what is known
as 'television,' not only among media researchers but also in the
television industry. Furthermore, this conceptualisation in many ways
permeates the cultural and industrial politics regulating the industry,
as well as the conceptualisation of 'television' among individual producers and audiences. Because the schedule performs five communicative functions fundamental to television it is able to serve as a prism
of change. Running through this book's case studies is the question
of how the present industrial volatility is managed and put into communicative practice in the production of the schedule as a genre. The
context is the very small and highly digitally evolved Danish market
of 5.6 million people defined by a strong take up of OTTs and social
media. It is furthermore defined by two dominating and popular public service television companies and a strong cultural-political tradition of securing Danish-language content production in all television
genres and subject areas, and with the explicit remit to use relevant
media platforms in order to reach the audience. The overall answer to
this question is that despite these conditions that are supporting the
development of a non-linear television paradigm the linear television
paradigm is still very powerful and of great importance to the genre
and its production. This is the case even if non-linear strategies are
being appropriated and given high priority from within the companies, and especially by the two public service companies. The patterns
in this, in many ways, 'extreme case' of the highly digitalised Danish
television industry are therefore of general value to scheduling studies
and to television studies in general because the contextual features in-
tensify fundamental issues also found, for example, in larger markets
with a more dominant private television sector, less digitally evolved
markets and markets less defined by the cultural-political governance
of the television industry.

In Chapters 3 and 4 the features of the third tier of the schedule,
the on-air schedule and the bits between the programmes known as
'continuity' were the focus of the analysis. In Chapter 3 the differences
in communicative strategies, identity branding and conceptualisation
of the audience between two public service companies were presented
and discussed. The analysis pointed to the conservative influence of
commercial funding (commercials and subscriptions) compared to a
licence fee or tax model. In combination with a platform neutral public service obligation to cater to the audience the latter funding model

seems to be a huge advantage to public service television in the digital era. The tax funding of the Danish Radio and Television Company (DR) is much more oriented towards 'herding' the implied viewer towards other 'places' in the portfolio compared to TV 2, and DR has developed trailing practices and promotional strategies in 'continuity' that sets the company apart from its competitors. In short, DR is in a much better shape to embrace non-linear user habits and adapt its communicative strategy in scheduling to both modes of watching television.

The conservative influence of a traditional commercial funding model on the communicative strategies was further explored in the analysis of the implied viewer of 'continuity' across public service and commercial television. Especially the commercial television companies cling to a very traditional communicative strategy of delay and procrastination with a focus on keeping the implied viewer on their main linear channels. Compared to the two public service companies this means that the communicative strategies are very different. This conceptualisation of the viewer might run into problems with the audience in the digital era: the audience's expectations regarding access to audio-visual content are presently influenced by forms of entertainment where waiting for content and the experience of personal agency is very different compared to the communicative traditions inherited from the linear television paradigm. However, this presumed impatience of the audience is counterbalanced by the resilience of the communicative strategies of 'continuity' across public service and commercial television, and this conservatism might be connected to communicative qualities found in the genre associated with the experience of watching television. As pointed out, the genre is able to produce the experience of sociability, immediacy and 'live-ness,' and these experiences of relational qualities are difficult, or perhaps even impossible, to get from the interface of a streaming service with no such para-social dimensions. The conservatism found in these communicative strategies might therefore be a consequence of a genre interpretation among the producers that gives priority to such qualities.

In Chapters 5 and 6 the production of the on-air schedule and 'continuity' for commercially funded public service television on the small Danish market was in focus, and TV 2 the case. The findings in these two chapters also underscore the conservative influence that the traditional business model in the television industry has on the practices in the production culture at TV 2. In Chapter 5 the findings show that the digital era and the tensions between the two televisions paradigms have supported and increased the importance of the linear schedule. At TV 2 a strong main channel in terms of audience ratings and shares is of the essence in the TV 2 ecosystem. Currently this means that the economic importance and the promotional value of the linear main channel are actually growing. This development supports the increasingly powerful position of the schedulers within the organisational hierarchy and their editorial power in order to follow this trajectory. The role of 'continuity' in branding the cultural values of the main channel is paramount and exhibits a conceptualisation of the audience imbedded in alleged core company values at TV 2. At the same time the schedulers are trying to flesh out how the linear and the non-linear distribution modes of the content can produce synergies as well as cater to the two modes of watching television, respectively. The lessons learned so far suggest that Danish-language content is of increased significance to both modes of watching television in the digital era. Specific genres, narrative formats, emotional relations and values seem to travel across both modes as well, and these are important to the strong emphasis on the streaming service in the company's portfolio and in order to meet its public service obligation. This growing dependency on the main channel and its interplay with the streaming service produce dilemmas when it comes to scheduling for a young audience, which is an economically and politically important segment for the television industry to cater to.

Chapter 6 addresses these problems in the production culture at TV 2. The importance of the in-house streaming service TV 2 Play is growing rapidly in terms of organisational focus, and the scheduling and curation strategies at the streaming service are increasingly directed at the younger segments of the audience. However, the production practices of linear scheduling for this target group are in conflict with the needs detected to schedule the streaming service in order to retain and attract young viewers. Furthermore, the economic and promotional dependency on the linear youth channel TV 2 Zulu is a conservative influence on how TV 2 navigates, even if the resources to produce more content for the linear channel are not the priority. In short, the target group of 15–39-year-olds has to be catered for within the present resources. However, the target group prefers Danish-language content in expensive genres: fiction, comedy and reality programmes, and it is a very small segment of the already small Danish audience. All in all, the practices of scheduling a low-budget niche linear channel are problematic and produce problems to the otherwise acknowledged synergies between the linear and non-linear modes of watching television that the schedulers currently try to cultivate. The mushrooming of linear niche channels since the late 1990s in the television industry and the segmentation of the audience following this survival strategy have probably come to their definitive termination, given these new challenges. Instead, and building on the findings in this book, a focus on popular main steam channels with strong channel identities combined with a sophistication of the streaming services in terms of target groups and personalisation tools might be the new strategy in the industry in order to meet economic and cultural-political demands.

The digital television paradigm

In the rest of this concluding chapter I argue that the contours of *a third television paradigm* are being produced by the new scheduling practices from within the multi-platform television organisations themselves in order to adapt to the tensions between linear and non-linear television and to address the changing viewer habits. I term this paradigm 'digital television,' and Table 7.1 sums up its features in line with Table 1.1 presented in Chapter 1.

I use the term 'digital television' to conceptualise the current development in scheduling instead of 'online TV,' as suggested by Johnson, covering all kinds of editorial audio-visual content distribution via the public internet (2019: 30). The emphasis in Johnson's definition is primarily put on the internet as the infrastructure for distribution of television content, and not on the technology involved. Even if the access to 2.0 high-speed internet is essential to the current developments in the television industry and the emergence of transnational providers of audio-visual content like Netflix, digital technology is the fundamental driver. It is involved in all stages of television, from the production to the distribution and the consumption of content providing

Table 7.1 A digital television paradigm

Television paradigm	Digital
1: Consumption	Production for multiple localities and digital devices: content and distribution
2: Viewer access	Two modalities of access available
3: Communication	Mass interactivity
4: Textual characteristics: distribution	Merger between linear and non-linear distribution both mirroring and structuring the time structures and routines of everyday life in specific socio-cultural context
5: Textual characteristics: content	Merger between temporal and spatial logics to fit linear schedules and non-linear databases

this kind of television with fundamentally different cross-media and communicative possibilities compared to those available to analog television. The term also acknowledges the different forms of digital distribution *not using the internet* still hugely important to the television industry, e.g. the cable companies as well as the private and public digital terrestrial television (DTT) operators acting as intermediaries as well as competitors in the economic value chain of the industry. As pointed out in Chapters 3–6 the role of these stakeholders is extremely important in order to understand how the schedulers navigate, and this will probably influence the development of television in the foreseeable future.

The overall characteristic that defines this emerging digital television paradigm is first and foremost *the merger* of the traditional linear television paradigm and the disruptive features of the emerging non-linear television paradigm. In the practices of the schedulers the sharp distinction between the two does not really apply to what scheduling is, and this epistemological approach can also be applied to what television is becoming, e.g. in terms of consumption of television content is no longer only taking place on a television-set, and the private sphere of the audience is no longer the only arena where the content is performed. For example, a new episode of a drama series can be watched on your phone while sitting on the train to work, and the digital television paradigm is increasingly focussed on content and different modes of distribution, at least in principle. At the same time the developing scheduling practices continue to suggest that the majority of television consumption is still taking place in the private sphere, e.g. the home, and in the leisure time even if the content is accessed from a multitude of devices. In Denmark the use of television is still very intense in the evening and this pattern has to do with the fact that most women work outside of the home, and young children (in 2019 it was 9 out of 10) are placed in child care centres during the day. These traditional ways of consuming television make it an audio-visual medium that continues to bridge public and private life. Its genres and modes of address continue to be embedded in specific socio-cultural contexts and concrete physical places like the living room, as Scannell argues (1996: 21). This merger of the linear and the non-linear and the resilience of the traditional patterns of consumption framing the communicative characteristics of the schedule and the practices of scheduling point to a more general *second issue* of how media development is understood and conceptualised in television studies. The findings speak to an anything but a development towards a kind of non-linear take-over of television. Instead they foreground a much more complex and multidirectional development where technology is not the only change producing driver. As Amanda Lotz argues a medium is 'a social construct' of textual characteristics, industrial practices, audience behaviour as well as socio-political context and national media history (2014: 7). In the Nordic context it is important to acknowledge how the cultural-political ambitions regarding television are of great significance to how technological innovation is implemented. In other parts of the world the market forces may lead the development to a much higher degree.

The merger of the linear and the non-linear defining digital television means that viewer access to content is conceived as a choice between two modalities of television viewing: linear or non-linear, driven by the needs of the audience. As documented the schedulers are trying to flesh out and understand the differences and the interconnections between these two modalities. A *third issue* to be considered based on this development concerns television's continued importance as a cultural phenomenon (Meyrowitz 1985) embedded in the everyday life of the audience. First, the possible experience and indeed emotional qualities of watching linear television need to be taken into consideration when discussing the future conceptualisation of the medium. Second, as pointed out by Johnson (2019: 31) the concept 'online TV,' or 'digital television,' as I would rather term it, must not be conflated with time shifted television. Most streaming services provided by the incumbent television companies, at least in the United Kingdom and in the Nordic countries, integrate linear and non-linear access, and watching linear television is possible through live streaming. So-called simul-cast of a linear schedule continues a very traditional mode of watching television despite the device and distribution technology used to access the content. In other words, the linear and the non-linear are mixed and accessible alongside each other in the digital era even if the television and the internet are technologically intertwined in terms of distribution and the devices. Furthermore, the linear viewing mode of content is still preferred in Denmark. In 2018 only 9 minutes out of 2 hours and 22 minutes of daily viewing were spent on non-linear use (Kantar Gallup viewer data, authors' analysis, May 2019). Furthermore, 50 per cent of the time spent on TV 2's streaming service TV 2 Play is used watching a linear television (Head of Scheduling TV 2 Mette Rysø Johansen 23.4. 2019; Head of TV 2 Play Content Sune Roland, 9.4. 2019, personal interviews). And as a sign of the continued strengths of the linear paradigm HBO Nordic is currently appropriating classic scheduling tools, e.g. the new episodes of the third seasons of the series *The Handmaid's Tale* and *Big Little Lies* are scheduled on Mondays and Thursdays. The conflation of technology, the devices involved as well as the social use of television need to be avoided because it may cloud the important changes and not least continuities that need to be considered in television studies if the goal is to re-conceptualise what television is.

However, in a digital television paradigm, television can certainly not be defined by the devices for access to the content and has to be based on how the companies 'construct a service focused on facilitating the viewing of editorially selected audiovisual content,' as Johnson argues (2019: 30). Among the schedulers the two modes of watching television are increasingly regarded as interconnected, mutually interdependent and able to produce synergies that are securing high ratings. In doing so the 'broadcastification,' or linear scheduling, of the streaming service is evident. As pointed out in this book, television fiction, documentaries, factual entertainment and reality shows in Danish are genres creating these synergies at the moment; however, specific genres are still preferred as live broadcasts only. Transmissions of sports are at the top of the chart, and breakfast television shows, news talk shows as well as the news are doing well too. And finally, specific genres, or more likely specific programmes, only do well on streaming. To sum up, the streaming service application on a smart TV or a mobile phone could be regarded as a kind of 'front door' (Grainge and Johnson 2018: 28) to the entire portfolio in the future. However, as pointed out in this book, getting access to the portfolio through cable or the DTT network still remains preferred by the industry for economic reasons. These cultural-political, and not least economic, dimensions are perhaps becoming more important to what television is in different national and regional contexts. This increasing diversification of television speaks to the continued importance of the cultural embeddedness of television and the need for a non-universal epistemological conceptualisation of the medium.

The merger of the linear and the non-linear defining the digital television paradigm presently produced by the scheduling practices questions what kind of communication is on offer. In the linear television paradigm one-way mass communication was the technological default setting whereas a non-linear television paradigm holds the promise of interactivity. The digital television paradigm produced by the incumbent television companies seems to be very much dominated by the traditional mass communicative approach, and only to a very limited degree by cultivating a personalised approach. As documented in Chapters 5 and 6, the use of algorithmic prediction and recommendation systems is currently not very advanced at TV 2 and this low level of implementation is supported by the finding in Kirk Sørensen and Hutchinson's work based on interviews with key professionals at public service companies in ten European countries during 2016 and 2017 (Kirk Sørensen and Hutchinson 2017). As pointed out in Chapter 2 there are different sources of knowledge about the audience available to the schedulers, and the use of Artificial Intelligence (AI) systems and digital personalisation by streaming companies is pushing the traditional broadcasters in the same direction. Currently, the kind of viewer data that is including seven days of streaming into the ratings is, nevertheless, the most important tool in the work of the schedules in combination with data analysis of the subscribers' behaviour on the company's in-house streaming service. The present use of collaborate filtering algorithms is still very limited but is regarded as a future possibility for public service television to stay relevant and in touch with its audience's taste, interests and expectations towards access to television content. The focus is very much on retaining specific profitable and politically important target groups and taste communities. The traditional demographic and lifestyle segmentation tools based on statistics in various combinations with collaborate filtering algorithms are probably the kind of communication on offer in a digital television paradigm, hence the term 'mass interactivity' in Table 7.1. However, in order to match the industrial discourses on how the use of the steaming services, there is a growing need in television studies for publicly available viewer data that includes these streaming services. To open this in many ways, new 'black box' about the use of television, television studies needs access to viewer data on the use of the in-house streaming services that are dominated by public service content, which is currently not measured by the available viewer ratings. In short, the transparency in how public service television content is used need improvement.

This feature of the digital television paradigm concerns the conceptualisation of the audience and involves the discussion of a *forth issue*: the survivability of public service television. The findings in this book point to its ability to adapt, even if the inherited commercial business models from the traditional linear television paradigm are a conservative force that limits the manoeuvrability of commercially funded public service companies like TV 2. The schedulers have the advantage of knowing the local audiences very well. Currently, they draw on this accumulated professional knowledge in the editorial processes, as pointed out in Chapters 5 and 6, e.g. in reorganising the scheduling seasons to better accommodate the needs of the streaming service or in giving priority to specific programmes in order to avoid growing churn rates. In this way the merger of the linear and the non-linear scheduling practices is still mirroring the rhythms and routines of everyday life in specific countries. In the case of TV 2, the temporal structures of traditional broadcasting are mirrored by the editorial layout of TV 2 Play and well-known scheduling tactics and tools are being challenged as well as cultivated to fit the needs of the merger. Furthermore, as Chapters 3 and 4 have documented a tax funding public service company, like DR, with platform neutral obligations has the agility to adapt its schedule to a multi-platform and non-linear distribution mode, and this agility speaks to the adaptability and pragmatic resource in the company. In Denmark, both public service television companies are doing really well in terms of audience share compared to the commercial companies. This continued popularity might be connected to the final feature of the digital television paradigm presented in Table 7.1: the textual characteristics of the content. Within limited resources the creative interest is merging the two temporal logics of content and narrative formats in order to fit time-structured schedules, with standardised slots as well as the streaming service. The need for prized content in Danish is the big challenge, but a database of files in combination with linear schedules also represents the opportunity to develop new kinds of television content that does not have to fit the production standards of individual genres. The lack of time restrictions is of special importance to the schedulers' ability to accommodate the need for new content. However, the structural power of the linear paradigm is important and very much still in place in the industry. The revenues from the subscriptions to channel bundles and traditional spot commercials are essential to the economy in the industry. Especially in small markets with a high demand for local language production in all genres in order to compete for audiences this business model can easily turn into a problem, because television programmes cost the same to produce regardless of the size of the audience.

The merger between the linear and the non-linear that defines the contours of a digital television paradigm in many ways makes topical the *fifth and final issue* for discussion: the complex relationship between change and continuity in understanding what television is in the digital era. The challenge in a situation of perpetual change is how to distinguish between superficial and important changes? How does television studies avoid buying in to the industrial hype and the agenda of different stakeholders within and outside of the industry? And how does television studies manage to focus on what is actually going on that will be important to the role of the medium in society in the long run? The grand theories of television were argued when the linear television paradigm reigned supreme, and this is certainly no longer the case, but as several television scholars have pointed out, television has never been a particular stable phenomenon. As Enli and Syvertsen's article 'The End of Television – Again!' from 2016 suggests the present changes and the many predictions of an impending demise are just 'another day at the office' for the medium, and television studies needs to acknowledge that change is perpetual. However, according to Enli and Syvertsen four contexts are important in order to assess what this perpetual change brings along, and the analysis of television therefore needs to be 'localized' in order to make sense. These are the European media policy framework, the national arrangement of public service television, the welfare state and the media ecosystem. Enli and Syvertsen demonstrate the workings of these four contexts using the Norwegian television system as a case, and finally, the authors point to the importance of how the television companies respond to these contexts and they conclude:

> Even though the TV industry is currently undergoing significant changes, not least as a response to convergence and new digital intermediaries, these changes do not represent the full picture. In tandem with change and renewal, there is stability and continuity. Traditional TV is still an economic, cultural, and social important medium, and as pinpointed by Lotz (2014, p. 170) television remains an incredible profitable industry, yet not as profitable as before.
>
> (2016: 149)

In sum, the death of television-rhetoric is not supported by empirical evidence. William Uricchio (2013) argues along the same lines and points to the fact that presently the past of the medium is being frozen discursively in order to make a rhetoric point. The period serving as an apparently stable past is argued to be between 1950 and 1980 in the United States and Europe (Uricchio 2013: 65). Perhaps the medium's transformative abilities are in fact the key to its survivability and ability to stay culturally and politically relevant and popular in a society. The schedule and the skill of scheduling play no small part in these abilities. Furthermore, and for many good reasons, television studies tend to emphasise change rather than continuity. By doing so researchers might, nevertheless, pay too little attention to the complexity of media development. As this book has hopefully demonstrated continuity is a strong dimension in what is presently happening in the television industry, which influences the kind of television produced in the digital era.

References

Enli, G. and Syvertsen, T. (2016) The End of Television – Again! How TV Is Still Influenced by Cultural Factors in the Age of Digital Intermediaries. *Media and Communication*, 4(3), pp. 142–153.

Grainge, P. and Johnson, C. (2018) From Catch-up TV to Online TV: Digital Broadcasting ad the Case of the BBC iPlayer. *Screen*, 59(1), pp. 21–40.

Johnson, C. (2019) *Online TV*. London: Routledge.

Kirk Sørensen, J. and Huchinson, J. (2017) Algorithms and Public Service Media. In G. Ferrell Lowe, H. Van den Bulck and K. Donders (eds.) *Public Service Media in the Networked Society*. Gøteborg: Nordicom, pp. 91–106.

Lotz, A. (2014) *The Television Will Be Revolutionized*. New York: New York University Press.

Meyrowitz, J. (1985) *No Sense of Place*. New York: Oxford University Press.

Scannell, P. (1996) *Radio Television and Modern Life*. London: Blackwell.

Syvertsen, T., Enli, G., Mjøs, O.J., and Moe, H. (2014). *The Media Welfare State: Nordic Media in the Digital Age*. Ann Arbor: The University of Michigan Press.

Uricchio, W. (2013) Constructing Television: Thirty Years that Froze an Otherwise Dynamic Medium. In M. de Valck and J. Teurlings (eds.) *After the Break. Television Theory Today*. Amsterdam: Amsterdam University Press, pp. 65–79.

Index